"*Since Joel* is beautifully written, wi̇̇ ̸ ̸ ̸ ̸ ̸ ̸ ̸ ̸ Schwartz takes us to the depths of grief and allows us to understand its power and the courage that it takes to face it. Anyone who has ever lost a loved one will see the honesty in every line and will appreciate how Schwartz has put such raw emotions into words."

—MARINA NEMAT, AUTHOR OF
PRISONER OF TEHRAN AND *AFTER TEHRAN*

"As a parent of a son with autism, it was obviously an emotional rollercoaster—and her words were very relevant to the day-to-day experiences we 'special' parents share."

—DARREN WILLIAMS, CHAIRMAN OF THE BOARD OF
DIRECTORS OF THE GENEVA CENTRE FOR AUTISM

"*Since Joel* is told with brutal honesty about what it's like to raise a child with Autism Spectrum Disorder. It is a story about bullying, harassment, humiliation, and ostracism. Any parent with a challenged child should be interested and could relate to the experiences recounted in this book. There are different ways in which to process grief and this book provides a learning opportunity for anyone coping with life altering difficulties and loss."

—MARSHALL ROTHSTEIN, FORMER
SUPREME COURT OF CANADA JUDGE

"*Since Joel* is an affecting and affectionate remembrance of a mother yearning still for her different from all the rest and gone too soon and too painfully son. It's one mother's story, yet it belongs to every mother—Joel Schwartz was that memorable, and his mother Julie that good a writer."

—RABBI JOHN MOSCOWITZ, RABBI EMERITUS
OF HOLY BLOSSOM TEMPLE, TORONTO

SINCE JOEL

SINCE JOEL

LOVE AND LOSS ON THE SPECTRUM

JULIE L. SCHWARTZ

Second Story Press

Library and Archives Canada Cataloguing in Publication

Title: Since Joel : love and loss on the spectrum / Julie Schwartz.
Names: Schwartz, Julie, 1951- author.
Identifiers: Canadiana (print) 20190185112 | Canadiana (ebook) 20190185120
  | ISBN 9781772601237 (softcover) | ISBN 9781772601244 (EPUB)
Subjects: LCSH: Schwartz, Julie, 1951-—Family. | LCSH: Schwartz, Joel,
  1983-2009. | LCSH: Asperger's syndrome—Patients—Biography. | LCSH:
  Parents of developmentally disabled children—Biography. | LCSH:
  Mothers of children with disabilities—Biography. | LCSH: Children—
  Death. | LCSH: Parental grief. | LCGFT: Biographies.
Classification: LCC RC553.A88 .S39 2020 | DDC 616.85/88320092—dc23

Editors: Kathryn White and Kathryn Cole

Printed and bound in Canada

*Second Story Press gratefully acknowledges the support of the
Ontario Arts Council and the Canada Council for the Arts for our
publishing program. We acknowledge the financial support of the
Government of Canada through the Canada Book Fund.*

 ONTARIO ARTS COUNCIL
CONSEIL DES ARTS DE L'ONTARIO

 Canada Council Conseil des Arts
for the Arts du Canada

 Funded by the Government of Canada
Financé par le gouvernement du Canada |  Canada

MIX
Paper from
responsible sources
FSC FSC® C103567
www.fsc.org

Published by
Second Story Press
20 Maud Street, Suite 401
Toronto, ON M5V 2M5
www.secondstorypress.ca

SINCE JOEL *is dedicated to Joel David Schwartz;*
whose goodness outmeasured his years.

With genuine thanks to all who were kind to him; and
unending gratitude for everyone who reads his story and
honors his memory by being kind to those who are different.

AUTHOR'S NOTE
What's in a Name?

When our son was born, we named him Joel David Schwartz and assumed that was that. The older he got, though, the more labels he collected.

When it became obvious that he was atypical, an official label was required to access support services for him. At a very young age, he was assessed and deemed to have PDD-NOS, which stood for a Pervasive Developmental Disorder—Not Otherwise Specified. Then we were told he had autism. When he was six years old, he was diagnosed with a sub-type of autism called Asperger's syndrome, named for the Austrian doctor who first identified the condition as separate from high functioning autism.

For educational and school placements Joel was also variously labeled as having: a generalized learning disability, a non-verbal learning disability, a spatial learning disability, and/or a combination of gifted and learning disabled because of his pronounced strengths and weaknesses.

From our perspective, the label that best captured the constellation of characteristics Joel exhibited was Asperger's syndrome, which at the time his psychiatrist diagnosed him, was listed in the Diagnostic and Statistical Manual (DSM).

Since Joel's death in 2009, disability politics, the scientific community, and newly unearthed negative information about Dr. Hans Asperger have called into question the use of the name Asperger; and the newest DSM has dropped the diagnosis in favor of the more generalized: Autism Spectrum Disorder or ASD.

I am happy to see these terms evolve with our changing knowledge. In this memoir you will see a mix of older and newer language as I've tried to reflect both current usage and the terminology that was in place during the course of Joel's life.

THE VISIT

THANKS FOR COMING to visit me when we were up north, Joel. I didn't expect to see you so soon. You know, you really threw us for a loop when you left. Ernie had packages for you to deliver, and Dave said you guys were invited to a party. Well, anyway, your being away gave me a chance to go through your desk. I found the "Perfect Day" story you wrote for Ms. Rymal in grade three. In it, you wake up early and eat popcorn for breakfast, have hot dogs for lunch, and ice cream and fries for dinner. You have lots of friends and visit Wonderland on the GO bus. At the end, you come home, have M&M's for a midnight snack, and go to sleep in your own bed with your bear, Radar. The story is just like you, kiddo: honest, plain, and good.

Do you remember when we got our backyard tree house with the ladder up and the blue sliding board down? The first day we had it, Jason came over. He beat you to the top, shot down the slide, threw his hands up, and screamed, "The winner!" You came down next and yelled, "The loser!" and he got really pissed off because you were as happy to lose as he was to win.

Have you met anyone new? Maybe some nice people like the gang from your Israel trip who loved you just the way you are and were so pleased to have you with them on their journey? Any like the Camp John Island crew? I was so grateful that they included you, no questions asked. It was such a huge relief to know you had a fan club when you went to Sudbury. Hopefully you haven't run into too many like the jerks in high school who tied up your arms and hit you in the head with a soccer ball. I remember they called you "special in an Olympic way." I wanted to hurt them for hurting you…. And I really hated the ones at West Prep who promised they would be your friends if you ate pretzels out of the garbage and then laughed so hard when you did.

We still chuckle every time we get stuck in traffic on the way to the cottage and think of when you were little and asked if we were going to have peanut butter to go with the traffic jam we were mired in. You took everything so literally. Once when we were all in the bedroom, with Dad standing on one side of our bed and me on the other, you jumped in front of me when I asked Dad to toss me over my bathrobe. You had such a serious face when you warned Dad that I would get hurt if he tried to throw me over my robe because it was hanging high up on the closet door and I would fall so hard to the floor if he threw me over it.

Remember how clearly we could see Orion in the night sky? And that winter when Dad was in Uganda, I took you and Jonathan and Kimberly and Tyler to Viewmount Park to stargaze. We ran into Lewis, and he yelled at me for taking kids to a dark park at night and got so mad when you told him his dog, Ollie, looked like a cow. Dad and I once saw Orion when we were in Costa Rica. From there, he is turned sideways but you can still make him out. You taught us that Betelgeuse and Rigel are stars in his constellation. You told us that one is blue and one is orange, but I can never remember which is which without your help.

For the longest time, you only wanted to talk about constellations, trains and buses, and cell phones. Dr. Spring said it was called perseveration, and it was part of having Asperger's. You were like a miniature professor, and everyone was astounded by how much you knew. You drove Mel crazy begging to see his special walkie-talkie cell phone. He let you hold it but insisted that you couldn't touch any of the buttons because each one speed-dialed a different one of his workers. No matter how many times he told you that, you always were surprised and disappointed, and you always asked again.

Once, when I dialed Faigie's number, you said you could tell I was calling her from the sound of the beeps. You said her phone number always sounded like that. It reminded me of when you were about three and spelled words like yacht and surgeon, and when we asked you how you did it, you smiled and told us you had a word fairy deep inside your brain.

I don't know if you've seen it yet, but the new Canadian ten-dollar bill has a really cool image of the VIA Rail Canadian locomotive on the back. There is a huge renovation of Union Station going on, and soon the Canadian and all your favorite trains and Red Caps will have a new home. You knew the alabaster in the station walls came from Saskatchewan, and you once wrote a poem about how the main hall trestle looked like a cat arching its back. I used to worry that you'd get into trouble hanging around down there so much, but somehow it all worked out.

You aren't the only one obsessed with trains. Wasn't it amazing that night the Supreme Court judge came to our house for dinner? We said you could join us but could only ask two train questions. When your first one was whether he liked trains, Dad and I couldn't believe the judge told you he once worked on the Canadian and had specialized in transportation law. He knew more about the Park car than you did! After that, we couldn't get a word in edgewise. It was cool that you got to tell him about turning in that five hundred dollars in cash you found on your train trip to James Bay. The RCMP officer was right when he told you that the single mom who'd lost all her welfare money was lucky you were so honest.

As a matter of fact, there were times when you were *too* honest. You were thirteen when you wrote to us about your first girlfriend at camp. Two weeks later you called us to say she broke up with you and you couldn't figure out why...especially since it happened while you were telling her all the things you both had in common: that you loved swimming, sailing, cookies, and that you were both starting to grow moustaches!

Sometimes we talk about whether or not you left on purpose. Dad thinks you were being impulsive when Diana broke up with you that last time, but that you never really meant to leave. He says you had all your clothes and papers laid out and ready for work the next day. A lot has happened since you left. Lollie lived to be ninety-four years old. She died in her own bed, waiting for Debbie to reheat some chocolate pudding for her. Bubbie eventually moved to Pine Villa, and even though she couldn't remember how to make chicken soup anymore, she was happy. She lived to be the same age as Lollie and died peacefully. On January 27, 2018, Jonathan married his wonderful girlfriend, Jordanna. We know you would have loved her, and she would have loved you. Before he met Jordanna, Jonathan finished at McGill and went to Tel Aviv University to do a master's degree in Environmental Studies. When he came home, he and Zack and Jesse started the Joel Schwartz Memorial Hockey Tournament (JSMHT), and everyone gets free hot chocolate and popcorn just the way you did when you came to all Jonathan's games. They've raised tons of money for REENA to run programs that help people like you be included, just like you always wanted to be.

One of the initiatives is a brand-new kitchen that was renovated with funds from the JSMHT and serves as a vocational skills center and social purpose enterprise. I know you would have loved sampling the REENA BAKERS challah bread, doll.

When they realized that other people your age were leaving in the same way you did, Sunnybrook Hospital, where you died, created the Family Navigation

Program to guide people through the maze of mental health services and to try to prevent the kind of thing that happened to you. There's a photo of you on the director's desk, and under your picture is a message I think would make you smile. It says: STOP, and make no assumptions—LOOK, with unconditional positive regard—and LISTEN, as if a life depends on it... because it does.

SINCE JOEL

THIS IS WHAT has happened since Joel: since his birth, since his life, since his death, and on account of him.

I am sixty-five years old—five years younger than my father was when he had his stroke. He was a doctor, "an internist," as my mother used to say, and spent his entire life taking care of people: his parents, his sister, my mother and her seven siblings, my sister Lisa, me, and all of his many patients. He never went anywhere without his black bag of instruments and medicines. He was an anticipator, and his bag was always available just in case.

My father may be why I won't leave home without at least two Band-Aids, and he's probably why I pack a full first aid kit whenever we travel, even if it's only to go for a bike ride. After all, my dad knew you never know, and so do I.

Having spent a lifetime in temples of healing, my father understood it to be a complex and idiosyncratic process. Once, when Jonathan had an open wound, I learned about "healing through secondary intention." That's when there is a deep cut that is kept open so that the wound is forced to heal from the inside out and fills itself in all the way up to the surface. Rather than stitching the top edges back together, the cavity is urged to fill itself in to provide a more thorough and complete healing.

I think I have spent the past years healing by secondary intention, in some way coming to accept that the crevasse from Joel's death will have to fill itself in and sensing that suturing the top edges together would prove to be a tentative and unreliable fix. For some reason, the seventh year since Joel was the most difficult. I once read that phone numbers were originally designated to be seven digits because seven is part of the rhythm of human memory.

The first year after Joel died was the easiest. I hadn't absorbed what had happened and often replayed the day of his death as an episode of a television show presented in slow motion.

Remembering puts the one who remembers in charge. He or she can speed things up or slow them down, examine in detail or gloss over, compress or expand. I took comfort in how clearly I could conjure up an image of the dead Joel and remember thinking that as long as I could recall every detail of his dead body, I would always have him. If loss is not having Joel, then we didn't lose him, because he is with me all the time and often pops up in the most unexpected situations. The fact that he is dead and no longer here means he lost his life, but not necessarily that we lost him.

Once Joel left, friends, colleagues, and acquaintances were beyond sympathetic and supportive. The ones I liked were genuinely beside themselves, and those I didn't like still knew enough to get in on the action of comforting the bereaved mother, father, and brother. I was really feeling no pain but was simply puzzled by my new, nameless status. Not a widow, not an orphan, there is no official word for losing a child, and I often felt guilty about the attention. Joel was simply not around, yet everyone told me that I was amazing, strong, resilient, and brave. Secretly, I sometimes even felt proud. Once, during the Shiva, a neighbor made a strange comment in what must have been an effort to cheer me up. He told me he had never seen me looking better. Later on, when I glanced in the mirror, I could see that he was as correct as he was inappropriate. I felt no stress, had very few responsibilities, an easy way out of any obligations, and my days were all my own. For several years, I continued to be convinced that I had "done it" and had successfully lived through Joel's death. During the early years since Joel, I would periodically tell myself that if this was as bad as it gets, then I could handle it.

But anniversaries of his birthday, death day, funeral, unveiling, and yearly holidays without him mounted up and opened a gaping hole of grief. The death of a child presents the parents with a chronic illness. The distress can be managed, but flare-ups cannot be avoided. Mostly when the sadness rushed over the edge of the pit to trap me, I'd run like hell into fits of activity. Taking classes, walking for hours, making meals for homeless people, going to Israel to support victims of terror, sitting on charitable boards—anything to avoid sitting still with sadness.

Finally, when I couldn't run anymore, I allowed myself to stand in the muck of despair instead of trying to stave it off. Fleeing or sitting with it, kinetic or static, the same energy is spent. And once my shoes were muddy with sorrow, why avoid puddles? Why not go for it? Get in there and shuffle around in the sludge, and stomp and splatter it just to see how sad *sad* can be. How else to know where the bottom is without going there and hitting it hard? And then pile on self-pity by reviewing all the trophies that earn me that right: having a disabled child, being acutely aware of his unmet potential, bullying, missing out, always being at the back of the pack, left aside, not included, damaged goods, and after all that—losing that disabled son to death. It would be extraordinary if you could learn the lessons meted out by challenges without actually having to endure them…but of course, "you have to go through it to get to it." Not long after Joel died, I asked a woman who had lost her daughter if it ever gets any better. She told me it never gets better, but it does get different.

I recall all the little discoveries we made learning to live with Joel: the delight in uncovering the fact that I could imitate Big Bird and Snuffleupagus well enough to convince Joel to follow suggestions delivered in their voices and realizing just what a useful little engine Thomas the Tank Engine could be in terms of modeling appropriate social interactions. I got so good at intervening at every possible teachable moment that I didn't even realize when it was time to stop. As much as that all mattered then, it no longer does.

Joel's life was heroic in the smallest of ways. He

struggled every single day to make sense of the world. There are no medals for that. No hero's welcome home. No bravery beads. No honorable survivors of developmental disabilities or people who "fought DD bravely" but lost the battle. Simply, individuals and families who slug through each hour of each day and are then rewarded with the challenge/opportunity of doing it all over again. Just when Joel would finally get the hang of taking turns or putting himself in another's shoes or understanding an intangible concept, there'd be a change in the geography, the players, or the rules. And for all his progress, he'd be back at square one.

Right after Joel died, people told me they couldn't imagine what it would be like to lose a child. I told them that they actually could imagine it if they tried. I know because I used to do that. The only real difference is that when it is imagined, you can shake it off and continue living in the same way. Once it's happened, there's no shaking it off. Even a wound thoroughly healed by secondary intention bears a scar. To the people who kindly told us they could not imagine our pain, we said "Thank you." The difference between the real and imagined version is that the imagined one can be halted at any time, rewound to life, and stopped just before the real version. The actual version has no exits and goes on and on, and if you ever thought you'd gotten away even for just a minute, well then, some bird or bus or song or smell reminds you with a smack or a feather that you will never be able to forget. Somehow, hope is eventually transformed into the possibility of remembering in different ways.

What I now wonder is how much more difficult it might be to still be trying to manage Joel's life, or worse yet, being unable to manage it no matter how hard I try. Relegated then to the sidelines to helplessly watch him career out of control and crash and burn. In a strange and cruel way, his end spared me that nightmare. I know I am not defined solely by my son's death and that I exist in many incarnations and contexts. Shadows on white walls differ from those cast on the walls painted gray by grief. Preferring a white wall, but still prepared for shadows, I drag myself out of the muddy puddles, continue to make peace with relief, and try to share what's happened since Joel.

HAPPY BIRTHDAY

LOLLIE USED TO MAKE me laugh with stories about what it was like to be pregnant with me "in her tummy." My favorite one was about the night she and Pop-Pop were at a Philadelphia Orchestra concert and I kicked her so hard she landed in the lap of the lady sitting next to her. She and Pop-Pop had been married for ten years before I came along, and when I was born three weeks overdue, she reminded everyone that "it takes longer to build a Cadillac than a Ford."

Your dad wanted children before I did. I was scared to death about being pregnant and even more terrified about giving birth. I once saw Joan Rivers as a guest on Johnny Carson's *Tonight Show*. When Johnny asked Joan to explain to a man what giving birth actually felt like, she rolled her eyes and said in her thick-tongued New York accent, "Fuhrst take yah lowah lip and pull it out and up tuh touch yah nose...then, pull it up and ovah yah head tuh the back of yah skull..." Then she smirked into the camera and said, "So that's what givven burth feels like, Johnny."

I knew this was not for me. I didn't want to get fat, and I figured it would hurt like hell and that having kids would necessitate my own growing up. But Daddy eventually managed to convince me that we might be sorry once we were past the time when we could have children, and that it would be sad to miss such an incredible part of life. For the record, Dad actually can pull his lower lip up to touch the tip of his nose.

Eight years after getting married, "we" were pregnant. I don't recall much changing in the first few months. I felt thick and sluggish but otherwise okay. Dad and I decided to attend prenatal classes, and they were fun and funny. We were a pod of ever-larger beached whales with handlers. During a pelvic floor exercise, one woman announced that she would never wax her pelvic floor. Another expectant father wondered aloud if everything would continue to be his fault once the baby arrived. I kept trying to get someone, anyone, to describe exactly what the pain would be like, but the only thing people would say is, "Don't worry, you won't remember it once the baby is born." When the leader discussed inserting the epidural needle, I thought I would pass out. Needing a backup plan, I reassured myself that if things got too bad, I would just keep my legs crossed.

In the classes they tell you that labor starts when you "lose the mucus plug"—but they don't tell you what the mucus plug looks like. I pictured a small cork that would gently pop out to signal that things were underway. Not so fast or neat and tidy. Instead, after a few hours of what felt like menstrual cramps, I went to the bathroom and discharged a large gluelike viscous blob of gelatin. Certain I had given birth to a malformed fetus, I called the doctor crying. He reassured me that this was the mucus plug, agreed that the name was a misnomer, and asked Dad to time my contractions and bring me to the hospital when they were ten minutes apart. When I arrived, he suggested that I should tell everyone how nervous I was so that no one would mistake my ranting and raving for anger.

That evening, Dad walked and I waddled into St. Michael's Hospital, blathering to everyone that I was having a baby. Most just smiled. They had seen more than just a few like me. When we exited the elevator at the maternity unit, the Virgin Mary was there to greet us. She was serene in her pastel blue-and-white robe, and her feet were graced with floral gifts from the new babies' families.

I have a vague memory of us being ushered into a room that had a crucifix, a bed, and a bathroom that I raced into at each contraction. I remember eventually being extremely uncomfortable and pacing around the room trying to get rid of the pain. When it became a toss-up as to what would hurt more and longer, the anesthetic needle or stretching my lip over my head, I went for the epidural, and it worked. Or at least half of it did. One side of me was completely numb from the waist down, and the other side continued to feel wrenched and roiled by contractions.

At even intervals throughout labor, a nurse came in to track the maternal and fetal heartbeats and measure cervical dilation. Addressing me as Mrs. Schwartz, she asked if I would be more comfortable if the crucifix was removed. I think I asked her to leave it there because I needed all the help I could get. Since all was going well, she told Dad to get some rest because it would be his last for quite a while, and she promised she wouldn't let him miss the big moment.

Her visits were coming closer together. She would come in, take measurements, pat my belly, smile, and leave, saying she'd be back soon. She was a very kind nurse...until the next time she came in. Listening to the blimp that was my stomach, her face froze, and she turned into a crazed creature, racing out of the room screaming for a monitor and a doctor. She came flying back in with a machine and a resident trailing her. Two of them frantically tried to attach some little clamps to your head, which was still inside me. Instead, they managed to clip the clamps to the inside of my thighs.

Full-blown hysteria took over, and a high-pitched voice was bleating, "Where's my husband? Where's the doctor?"

The doctor was stuck on the Don Valley Parkway, and no one knew where Dad had gone to lie down. Announcing that they had "lost the fetal heartbeat"—*How can you lose a heartbeat?*—the nurse and the resident flew me into the delivery room. I was on a gurney, half lying down, half propped up on my elbows, pleading to see Dad and the doctor. The delivery team kept telling me to calm down, as if I might be able to do that: "Mrs. Schwartz, the baby is in distress and we need you to lie back and relax." *Oh sure, just give me a minute.* "We want to get the baby out as soon as possible." *Hmm, me too.* Then they said they needed to use forceps for the delivery.

I must have missed the forceps lecture in the prenatal classes. In my mind, I pictured them as the tongs you use to remove ears of corn from boiling water. Well, these were not tongs. The gowned, gloved resident approached me instead with a set of huge, construction-grade tools that looked like they could take ore right out of rock. They say that women forget the pain of childbirth and that the proof lies in all the second and third kids that get born. I can't recall anything between seeing the forceps and seeing you, but once I heard you cry, everything else disappeared.

Dad came rushing in as they were wiping you off, weighing you, and testing to ensure all was well. The doctor arrived right after that and in time to observe me delivering the placenta. He conferred with the nurse and resident about what he called "the little adventure" and mentioned that there was some calcification of the placenta that may have caused the loss of the fetal heartbeat for a bit. But he smiled, pronounced you a "good baby," reassured us that all seemed well, and we took him at his word.

That was April 29, 1983. Two days later we brought you home in a little yellow sweater and cap Bubbie had knitted for you. You always looked forward to celebrating your birthday, and you had that pleasure twenty-five times.

THE GOOD BABY

"MOMMY, was I a good baby?"

"Oh yes, doll. You were a wonderful baby. You were sweet and calm and cute, and you slept really well. Once, when Pop-Pop came to visit, you were sleeping so much that he held an ice cube on the heel of your foot to try to wake you up!"

"Did I pee and poo a lot?"

"I think mostly the normal amount. One time, Daddy was changing you, and you peed on him before he got your diaper done up. He was really surprised and told everyone that he was officially initiated into 'fathers of sons club.'"

"Did I burp and throw up?"

"Well, actually, you did for a while, but eventually

you outgrew it, especially after the doctor told us to put your crib mattress on a slant."

"Was I a crybaby?"

"No, really, not ever."

"Is that why you and Daddy decided to keep me?"

"JoJo, we kept you because we love you so much and we would never give you away."

"If you love me so much, then why did we have to get Jonathan?"

"We had Jonathan because we loved you so much that we wanted to have another child."

"When I was just born, did you and Daddy invite a man to come to our house and cut my penis like the man did to Jonathan last week?"

"All Jewish boy babies have a bris, Joel. Do you really remember yours?"

"No, but did I cooperate better than Jonathan did?"

"Well, Zaidy and Pop-Pop held you just like they held Jonathan. You did cry a little—most every baby cries 'cause it does hurt, but right after, the baby gets some wine and then some milk and then usually falls right to sleep."

"Mom, do you think Jonathan is a good baby?"

"I think so, what do you think?"

"I think he fusses too much, and his poop smells stinky—but Mommy, if you think he is a good baby, maybe we can take him back to St. Michael's Hospital, and they will just give him to another family looking for a good baby."

"But JoJo, he is *your* new baby brother."

"Mommy, he is NOT MY BABY. But I did have a funny dream about a baby...not our baby, but a different baby."

"Would you like to tell me about your dream?"

"Yes.... In my dream, a family had a baby.... Not our family, but a different family. And in the dream, the family was walking with the baby in a stroller.... Not our baby, but a different baby. And they were on a high-up path, and someone in the family, not me, Mommy, but someone ELSE, pushed the stroller off the path, and the baby fell down and died.... Not OUR baby but the baby in the dream."

"Oh, what a sad dream."

"No, no, no.... It was a happy dream because the baby didn't get hurt, it just died and went away, and then the family got back to normal."

"Mommy, my ear hurts again."

"Uh-oh, maybe another ear infection. Shall I call Dr. Lloyd?"

"Yes, it feels hot and it hurts and there's a song inside it."

"I just spoke to the nurse, and she says if we get to the office quickly, the doctor can see us before lunch. How 'bout I pack you a snack and you go put on your socks and shoes and wash your face."

"But he's gonna look in my ear not my face."

"Please, Joel."

"Okay, I'll get ready."

"You're such a big guy, I bet you can climb into the car seat all by yourself for me, and I will just buckle you in."

"Mommy, before we leave, I have a question."

"But JoJo, hurry up or we will be late."

"But Mommy, it's important."

(Backing out of the driveway now.) "What is your important question?"

"Mommy, are you sure you want to leave my new baby brother at home sleeping in his crib?"

WHITE COAT SYNDROME

ONCE, WHEN YOU were about three and a half years old, we bumped into your pediatrician at the supermarket. As he bent down to say hello, you cried and ran to hide behind the tomatoes. He was always kind and gentle when you went for check-ups, and he always had his nurse give the needles, so I couldn't figure out why you were so frightened.

"JoJo, say hi to Dr. Lloyd."

"It's not Dr. Lloyd!" you screamed.

"Of course it is."

"No, no, no! Dr. Lloyd wears a white coat and a funny necklace and he is where toys are…not near food."

The doctor was decent enough not to make an issue of your tantrum and left me to calm you down and finish shopping. I felt disheartened and embarrassed, though, and kept replaying the encounter in my mind. It finally came to me that your reaction was because you couldn't recognize Dr. Lloyd out of context. Up to that point you had only ever seen him at his office, so in your mind if he wasn't in his office wearing his white coat and stethoscope, then he couldn't be Dr. Lloyd—so of course, you were afraid of the supermarket stranger. Little by little, we learned to try to take things in the way we imagined you did. Without realizing at the time, we were attempting to "walk a mile in your shoes."

The next couple of times we had to go to the doctor, you continued to be so uncomfortable that Dr. Lloyd said he really couldn't assess how you were developing. He asked if he could make an appointment to come see you at our house, where he thought you'd be more at ease. I felt he was being devoted and diligent, and I was very impressed that he wore his white coat and stethoscope so you would recognize him. It worked, and you did.

When he arrived, you took his hand and led him to the playroom saying, "Come on down—spin and win!" Just like *The Price is Right* announcer, except in your own distinct twangy, high-pitched little voice. Then, you put a record on the turntable and sat transfixed, moving your head around and around in time with the orbit of the disk. I thought it was wonderful that you could entertain yourself so nicely.

Dr. Lloyd wanted to throw and catch the ball with you, but you weren't interested at all. When he tossed it, the ball hit you in the chest and rolled down to the floor, and you went back to the record player. I was pleased when he noticed the wooden block toy I had made for you so you could practice small motor skills. He told me it earned me at least a hundred and fifty "mommy points," but then he made some notes in his book when he saw that you couldn't do up buttons, un-latch the gate, or climb down the stairs using one foot after the other. Instead of alternating your feet, you had the cutest way of working both sets of your toes to the very edge of each stair and then jumping your feet down together to the next step.

When the doctor asked you questions, you replied by rhyming off all of our names and birthdays, rattling off the subway stations in order, and reciting your fa-vorite Thomas the Tank Engine story by heart. I smiled, thinking it was so cool that you could do all that. And I was especially proud when you showed Dr. Lloyd the front page of that day's *Globe and Mail*, pointed to each word in the headline, and asked him why the "Russians Invade Afghanistan." I remember smugly wondering how many other three-and-a-half-year-olds could do that. Apparently, not many. A little while later, when Dr. Lloyd said he wanted to discuss next steps, I really wasn't sure what he meant.

You were our first child, and Dad and I thought everything about you was wonderful and amazing. We assumed you were simply unusually smart, a little clumsy, and just had a funny way of talking. We noticed all your strengths and figured you'd eventually be able to do the things you couldn't do then. But Dr. Lloyd had seen hundreds of youngsters, and he knew something was wrong. So, "next steps" meant finding out what it was. He told us that your lack of eye contact, fascination with spinning objects, poor motor skills, and huge vocabulary but no interest in conversation indicated that you probably had something called PDD-NOS, aka Pervasive Developmental Disability-Not Otherwise Specified.

The strange letters and words loomed large and horrible and vague; and I was scared and shocked and hurt. A huge, amoebic, and unknowable enemy was suddenly hovering, and I didn't know how to protect you. The "not otherwise specified" part was the worst because that meant even the doctors didn't know what it was. I was so worried and angry that when Dr. Lloyd said he wanted to arrange for you to have some tests,

I said we wanted to arrange to find another pediatrician—but I didn't say it that politely. I actually told him to "fuck off and leave" as I showed him to the door.

I spent the next few months focusing intently on all the things you could do, ignoring all the issues Dr. Lloyd had pointed out. In desperate cahoots with denial, I made crossword puzzles for you to solve, which you did. I recorded you reading your favorite stories. I bought shoes with Velcro closings and clothing with elastic openings so no one could say you couldn't dress yourself. I even stooped low enough to make a deal with the Devil where I traded your unique talents in return for your being average.

Denial eroded. Reality set in, and I confronted the enemy and got to know it well. Research revealed that PDD-NOS was full of surprises, limits, talents, challenges, and questions, all of which were very interesting as long as they weren't attached to you. But as it turned out, many of them were. In fact, you demonstrated almost all of the hallmarks of this diagnosis. You were fascinated by weather phenomena, constellations, transportation, and geography. You showed an uncanny ability to absorb and retain factual information, memorizing train schedules, VHF frequencies, and alpha-numeric codes, yet you never once initiated a conversation other than to make a request. You would lock your eyes on specific items of interest, but rarely made eye contact with people. Amazingly, you could walk through a room containing only one chair and still bump into it, clearly lacking any sense of yourself in space. When Jeffrey's mom told me he had reassured her that he would not be the last to be toilet trained because you still wore diapers, my heart broke in half.

Finally realizing that we needed additional reinforcements, I screwed up all my courage and called Dr. Lloyd to apologize and ask if he was still willing to help us. He was gracious, accepted my apology, and said "yes." I told him I had behaved the way I did and threw him out of our house because I was hurt and frightened and wondered if he had any idea how he had made me feel. He said he understood and knew exactly how I felt.

"How is that possible? How could you have known how I felt when you told me Joel had PDD-NOS?"

"I know because I have a Joel."

Dr. Lloyd provided us with years of excellent medical care and wonderful empathetic support. It was through him that we came to know Joel's amazing eye doctor, ENT physician, psychiatrist, and dentist, all of whom showed what was possible through dedication, patience for one's patients, compassion, and positive regard. Along with Dr. Lloyd, Drs. Pashby, Smitheringale, Spring, and Geller were all in my dad's mold, and so they represented for us the very best examples of "first do no harm" and then do the best you can.

FIRST TIME LOST

SOME PEOPLE SAY that people with autism live in their own world in their own way, but people with Asperger's live in *our* world in their own way. When you were little, one of your own ways of living in our world was your obsession with anything round. You were a knobby-kneed, curly-haired imp, mesmerized by anything that resembled a wheel. If it went in circles, you adored it.

One rainy day, you were in the family room with your record player, and I noticed your head was moving 'round and 'round as you watched more than listened to the songs. By the tenth time "The Wheels on the Bus" rang out, I was convinced I had to break the cycle or lose my mind.

"JoJo, let's get in the car and go to the mall."

"Can I watch the wheels on the car?"

"You can see them when we get outside, but it's raining too hard to stand and watch them."

"But I want to see them go around."

"Joel, the rain will make you all wet if you don't get right in the car, and besides, it's not safe."

"Mommy, I want to see them go 'round and 'round…please."

"Will you stand on the lawn and not move?"

"Yes."

"Do you promise?"

"I promise."

Nothing moved forward when you got anxious or fixated on an interest. Frayed nerves along with trial and error showed me just how much I was willing to risk and what kinds of deals I could concoct in order to alleviate whatever was upsetting you. I hated the judgmental parental stares and whispers that came as part of the territory whenever I would try to calm you down by giving in to one of your unusual obsessions. On this day, no one was looking as I traded common sense for peace and allowed you to stand in the pouring rain, beside a moving car, so that you could watch the tires revolve as I backed down the drive. At the bottom, I braked, threw the car into park, jumped out, and scooped up my slippery, wet, delighted five-year-old and buckled you contentedly into your car seat. We drove off with you singing every verse of "The Wheels on the Bus Go 'Round and 'Round."

The mall came into sight. A welcome relief, I thought, ready for a reprieve. Not so fast. As we entered the underground parking lot, you squealed with delight as we circled 'round and 'round, descending to the third level. There, we found a spot and got out of the car. Your word fairy must have cued you, and you announced we were at Level 3, Section B-5.

"Can you please remember where we are parked, JoJo?"

"Yes."

"Hold on to my hand now."

"Mommy, look at all the wheels and tires here. Can we watch them go around?"

"Maybe later. Now that we're here, let's go to the store to buy you some new pants."

"But I don't want any new pants…. I want to watch the wheels."

"Pants first then you can choose: an ice-cream treat or wheel watching; but now, please hold my hand and let's go."

We arrived at the children's clothing department and found our way to the sale items. A half floor full of round, spinning display racks…merry-go-rounds of clothing. You broke my grip, beelined to the closest round rack, and began spinning and spinning it until clothes launched off it like colorful rockets flying into outer space.

"Joel, look at the mess you've made! You must stop right now and come help me clean up."

I grabbed your hand and dragged you with me while I tried to retrieve scattered clothing that had touched down in other departments.

"But Mommy, you giggled, it's so funny. Do you see those brown shoes? They are wearing the blue pants I spun off the rack!"

I actually chuckled, but only till you broke away again to play hide-and-seek among the spinning racks. You were the perfect height to blend in to the clothing as you bobbed and weaved your way from one to the next. Thinking we should have stayed home with your records, I decided it was time to teach you a lesson. *If you want to play hide-and-seek, I will play too. And when YOU can't find ME, then you'll be sorry.* I saw where you were hiding and tiptoed to the nearest rack. When you spied me, I crouched down out of sight for a few seconds. Then I popped up.

And you were gone.

I edged my way around the rack slowly, expecting

to see you beyond each curve. I reassured myself I would surely find you just past the next one. I crept three times around before panic grabbed me by the throat. You were nowhere in sight…an invisible five-year-old.

I pounced on the nearest sales clerk and choked out what had happened. Two security guards arrived and took a description of you. They said they would lock down the store, search the department, and inform mall security. They told me to stay where I was. My body stayed still, but my mind ran a marathon of bad thoughts. I winced with each new vision of someone tormenting or torturing you. I could almost hear you screaming for me while I was helpless to intervene. I tried to warn you not to be fooled by the man who promised you could pet his new puppy, but you were charmed and followed him. When he finished with you, he left you whimpering under a bridge.

My horror movie stopped when the mall security team arrived to say they had sealed off all mall exits and would begin a store-by-store and floor-by-floor search of the premises.

Not long after the guards left to coordinate the search an announcement came over the PA system. A voice called for "the mother of Joel Schwartz" to proceed immediately to the mall's main information desk.

I bolted there only to have to produce identification

proving I was Mrs. Schwartz. Once free, I raced down the corridor and could see you holding hands with a mall guard and a petite woman. I was crying and panting so hard, I barely heard them explain that the woman found you on the way to her car. You were sitting on the floor of level three of the parking garage, right next to our car in Section B-5.

When she asked what you were doing there, you told her you'd lost your mom so you went to the car to wait for me. I thanked the woman, sobbed, and thanked her again, and then we both cried more. Even the mall guards got teary.

"Mommy, aren't you happy to see me?"

"Yes JoJo—I am so happy and relieved to see you!"

"Then Mommy, why are you and everybody else crying?"

At the time, I couldn't begin to respond with an explanation of the difference between happy and sad tears because I felt it was just too intangible a concept about feelings for you to understand. Much later you educated me about feelings by imagining them as inanimate objects:

"Mom, do you remember that day when I was little and we each had an anger ball?"

"You mean when you were eight years old and I was screaming at you...and in the midst of sobs and blubbering you called me out for losing my temper, telling me you could see that I had an anger ball and it was red and yellow with orange spiky flames shooting out of it? You said you had one too, and that it was dark gray and black and filled with clouds of stinky smoke. I was so frustrated with you that I stormed out the door to make sure I wouldn't hit you. You followed me out on the front porch and grabbed my hand and said you had an idea. You pointed at the garbage can and told me you would throw your anger ball into it if I would throw mine in first. I couldn't believe you said that. You insisted that I go first because you were afraid of my anger ball. Slipping from fury to intrigue, I went to the garbage, lifted the lid, and pretended I was heaving a thirty-pound medicine ball into it. You smiled and imitated what I did. Then you put the lid back on, and we had a hug."

"Mom, you remember why you got so mad at me?"

"Because Mrs. Nicholls told me you were eating pretzels out of the playground trash can, and the other kids were making fun of you."

"But they said they would be friends with me if I ate out of the trash. You told me I had to learn to make friends by doing things that other kids want to do instead of only playing with my trains and buses."

"That's what made me so angry."

"Because I did what other kids told me to do? Were you upset with me or them?"

"With you and them. With them for setting you up, and with you for falling for it."

"I know I got a lot of things wrong—not on purpose, I just couldn't seem to help myself. I really did try my best almost all the time."

I think that's what upset me the most…realizing that your very best was never going to be good enough. Forget adjusting expectations. Forget being grateful for what you could do. It seemed that the balance sheet was always based on what you couldn't do, and that meant your future and ours would be all about not meeting the bar. No matter how much progress you made, each time you did something inappropriate, it offered further proof of failure and sent us all hurtling backwards. And we were already far behind. The crazy thing was that the more progress you made, the bigger the gap grew. Other kids were traveling at light speed, so the older you got, the more out of reach catching up became.

"Mom, were you more angry or more scared?"

"I think I was angry at the world and scared for you and us. I swung between hope and fear and anger and truth and lies. I wanted you to feel you could do anything you set out to accomplish. I had hope because almost everything we tried did help you grow. But then, with each new challenge, your achievements seemed to fade, and I could never really relax or catch my breath thinking you would be okay. I couldn't muster the confidence that you would do what any given situation called for, but I lied and told you I believed you could…. I thought I was trying to convince you, but now I know I was trying to persuade myself, too. What about you? More angry or more scared?"

"I think I was mostly confused. Anything new made me really nervous because nothing was ever the same and the rules always seemed to change. And I couldn't figure out what people were going to do next, even when I saw them do the same thing over and over…. I tried hard to do what I saw them doing because it seemed to work, but I don't think I ever got it quite right. Doing what I saw them do never got me where they seemed to be. I couldn't do it the same way as them. I could only do what they did in my own way. I think maybe the reason I like trains and buses so much is because they run on schedules and don't change their minds. You kind of always know what they're going to do next."

SHOW AND TELL

"YOU WANT some cookies." Your voice, eyebrows, and light-brown curls bounced with each word.

"No I don't, sweetie."

"Yes, yes, you DO." Your eyes brimmed. "PLEASE, you want just one!"

You cried until I remembered that *you* was *I* to you and gave you a cookie. You sniffled and smiled and wolfed down the cookie. Then, just as I had been taught, I put my face next to yours in profile and quietly explained: "When JoJo talks about JoJo, he says 'I.' So if JoJo wants a cookie, he says, 'I want a cookie, please.'"

The therapists said that inverting pronouns the way you did was just another symptom of an autism spectrum disorder (ASD) and indicated your difficulty in distinguishing yourself from other people.

Eventually you got your pronouns right, and we got used to it being just one more thing that made you unusual. Another trait that set you apart was your astounding vocabulary at a very early age. No one else's three-year-olds were asking, "How come it says Vaseline Intensive Care Lotion on the side of that bus?"

Meanwhile, for all your words, you almost never started conversations with kids your own age and rarely ever even spoke with them. In the language of assessment, it went like this: "Joel does not use the pragmatics of language to facilitate peer interaction." That's when I realized my main mom-job was to "facilitate peer interaction," and to do that meant we needed to have more kids around. A mom around the block told me that the best way to collect kids was to have the biggest cookie jar in the neighborhood and always keep it full of the best cookies. I bought a large, sturdy glass canister with a heavy lid, red rubber seal, and the capacity to house about three dozen cookies. I stocked it with Mr. Christie's newest Soft and Chewy Chocolate Chip Cookies, and when kids came over, we practiced letting each of them take a cookie before you, taking one cookie at a time, and selecting your cookie by putting your hand, and not your face, into the jar.

You always loved playing with words and making us laugh, and you often made terrific puns.

"Mommy, do you know how you can fix a traffic jam?"

"How JoJo?"

"Just add some peanut butter!"

"Mom, do you know where you can get the best meal in Ontario? In Kitchener! Dad, which U.S. state has the most writers? Pencil-vania!"

When you weren't making us chuckle or driving us crazy with other questions, you showed us how tricky the world can be when you don't fit in.

"Joel, have you decided what you would like to take to school for show-and-tell tomorrow?"

"One of my smoke detectors."

"Isn't there anything else you could share with the class?"

"No. I want to take the newest detector in my collection."

"JoJo, the kids may tease you if you bring that."

"Why?"

"Because most children don't collect smoke detectors. Other kids will be bringing in toys or stamps or baseball cards or dolls.... They might think it's really weird to bring a smoke detector."

"I don't care what they bring. I want to show my new detector. I like it 'cause it's round."

Poor Mr. G had yard duty on the day you brought the thing to school for show-and-tell. He was a grade six science teacher who wore a white lab coat and had a real reputation for being strict.

I had just finished cleaning up from breakfast when the school office called to say they needed me to come in because you and Mr. G were involved in an incident. I dropped everything and raced out the door and down the block. As I got closer to school, I could hear you screaming: "GIVE IT BACK, GIVE IT BACK.... It's mine for show-and-tell, and I can't go into school without it." I ran toward your voice and found a crowd of people gathered at the playground entrance. Mr. G was on the top step, and you were on the one below. He was holding your brand-new smoke detector, and you were wailing.

I worked my way up to where you two were standing, announced that I was your mother and, as calmly as possible, asked what was going on. Stating the obvious, Mr. G yelled to me that you had brought a smoke detector to school and that he was not going to allow you to bring it in because it was radioactive. "But we have them in our house," I said. I continued with our standard two-minute explanation for your fascination with round objects, only to be told that he was not about to allow your special needs to jeopardize the safety of other students and staff, most of whom had now congregated to take in the show. I only wanted to tell Mr. G how lucky he was that you didn't bring the rotating blades from our Mixmaster for show and tell.

Luckily, Mr. Chown, the principal, arrived on the scene.

"Mr. G, what seems to be the problem?"

"Joel is trying to bring a smoke detector into school."

"Hmm, I see. Other than being a little unusual, is this a problem?"

"Yes, it is, because smoke detectors are radioactive," pronounced Mr. G.

"They are?"

"Yes, they contain radon..." but when he tried to go on, you hijacked the conversation and explained exactly how the thing worked, leaving Mr. G and Mr. Chown and everyone else speechless.

First to recover, Mr. Chown mused to Mr. G that if the school had smoke detectors installed in the building and students had daily exposure to them, why not let Joel bring his smoke detector into school, but only for the grade one show-and-tell period, of course. As Mr. G clenched your smoke detector and tried to bolster his position, you continued crying. Mr. Chown suggested that maybe just this once an exception could be made and that "Mom can wait in the hall and take the detector home as soon as Joel finishes his presentation to the class."

The wisdom of this Solomon prevailed, and Mr. G backed down. I thanked Mr. Chown, who went on to run interference for you for the rest of your time at West Prep. Waiting outside Mrs. Nicholls' grade one classroom, I could hear your show-and-tell smoke detector lecture. Once you finished and handed the thing over to me for safekeeping, I was able to chuckle over the absurdity of the situation.

As it turned out, once Mr. G got to know you better, he became fascinated with your ability to consume and retain facts, and your unique nonjudgmental perspective on other human beings. He even became a fan and allowed you to hold the key collection he kept on his big FORD F-150 ring.

When I was in grade one, I had a collection of shells that I inherited from one of our neighbors. It had lots of unusual conch, crab, and oyster specimens, and each one had been stuffed with cotton and then glued into its own individual compartment in a huge cigar box. I remember I got rave reviews when I shared it with my class, and from then on, I always tried to bring the most interesting thing I could find for show and tell. My efforts caught Pop-Pop's attention, and one time he offered a suggestion.

Sunday was the only day he didn't go into the hospital to make rounds and check on his patients, so that was the day Auntie Lisa and I got him all to ourselves. Lollie would go out with her girlfriends to eat fried clams with tartar sauce at Howard Johnson's, and Pop-Pop would stay with us. Sometimes he took us on adventure hikes at Valley Forge, and we would find old musket balls from the Revolutionary War. Other times we would stay in and listen to him play the piano. One time, he showed us how to recreate some toys and tricks he used to make as a boy.

That Sunday, he picked Lisa and me up from Hebrew school, surprising us with a red inflated helium balloon bouncing and floating around in his car. We were delighted and giggled as we grabbed at the string to try to keep it still so he could drive. When we got home, we tied the string around Lisa's finger and carefully brought the balloon inside. Pop-Pop sent us around the house to collect a paperclip, bobbie pin, tissue, and pencil; and he told us to meet him in the sunroom.

Setting the balloon free from Lisa's hand, and holding the string himself, he explained that the challenge was to figure out which item to attach to the balloon's string so that the whole contraption would hang in mid-air. We took turns, and Lisa started with the tissue, which proved to be too light because the balloon floated up to the ceiling. When it was my turn, I tied on the pencil, and the balloon sank. The bobbie pin and the paper clip were neck and neck, but after three tries, it was clear that the bobbie pin was slightly heavier. The paper clip yielded the "eureka" moment when, with it attached to the string, the balloon hung poised between the ceiling and the floor. We proved that gravity is a powerful force and found out that balance is difficult to achieve, let alone maintain. I mesmerized my classmates when I performed the experiment for them in show and tell; and I won first prize for my presentation.

All these years later, I often feel like a paperclip tied to the string of a helium balloon. No longer tethered by Joel's special needs, I am free to float up and away, until I bump into the ceiling that is his death, descend again, and hang suspended in mid-air. When I am poised there alone, I sometimes think about irony and paradox, those twin tricksters that informed Joel's life and ours. As for irony, well, how ironic is it that the simple addition of the letter y changes the most immutable element on the periodic chart and turns dependable iron into a word that actually describes a situation where the opposite of what you are expecting happens?

And how paradoxical is it that Joel's disability was so rooted in a disordered perception of space and yet he could read and interpret maps like a professional and, without ever once needing one when he became a courier, navigated his way through the entire city of Toronto?

I am still left to wonder how he learned to ride a two-wheeler at five and was able to negotiate black diamond ski hills, but couldn't move through a room without taking down a chair or a person in the process.

BAR MITZVAH GIFTS

A FEW MONTHS before your Bar Mitzvah, I bumped into one of our rabbis. Hoping to say something intelligent, I tried to form a sentence about what a perfect Torah portion you were scheduled to read because it was so full of relevance and meaning. But since rabbis make me nervous, I heard myself say instead, "Rabbi, Terumah is a really great portion." Smiling, he gently reminded me, "Julie, they are all great portions." That's why rabbis make me nervous.

You came to each "next step" in your life not quite ready. When the calendar called you thirteen, Judaism called you ready to become an adult. Thirteen was an age chosen in an era when lives where shorter and maturity was required earlier. The early Jews had good instincts; thirteen turned out to be half the number of years in your life.

As a life-cycle marker, the Bar/Bat Mitzvah symbolizes coming of age and being welcomed as a full-fledged member of the Jewish community. The ceremony itself includes a public reading of verses of the Torah corresponding to the Sabbath on which the Bar/Bat Mitzvah occurs. The young person may also prepare a D'Var Torah (a word of Torah)—an essay or speech expressing a personal interpretation of the text.

> The Torah portion for my Bar Mitzvah is called TERUMAH, and the theme of it is bringing gifts to the Temple to show the Jewish people's connection to God. The people were moving from place to place because they had just left Egypt. When they left Egypt, they found that God showed himself on Mt. Sinai. They were about to begin an odyssey, which would take them very far.

> My portion, especially the part about making a tangible connection, reminds me about how I stay connected with my interests and my family when they are not around. When I first went to sleep at away camp, my parents helped

me make a booklet with pictures of my family and my interests. We were very specific and included only those things that were most important and valuable to me, so that when I felt homesick, I could look at the exact things and people that I love.

Your inability to go beyond literal meaning saw you very fortunate to be assigned to read from Terumah and not from other portions about leprosy, menstruation, or war. Still, your concrete thinking posed a challenge when Dad and I tried to help you see Terumah's theme of gifts in its obvious metaphoric terms.

"Joel, what are your verses about?"

"Gifts the Jews were supposed to bring to God for the new tabernacle and God's instructions for how to build the tabernacle. It was measured in cubits."

"What kinds of gifts did God want?"

"Gold and Lapis Lazuli."

"Are there any other kinds of gifts?"

"I hope people will give me model trains."

"How about the kinds of gifts you can't see or touch?"

"Like, you mean, if someone deposits money into my bank account?"

"More like the gift you get from someone who

teaches you a lesson or shows you the right way to behave…. Could that be a gift?"

"I guess so."

"Do you think you could use your D'var Torah to share some of the gifts and lessons you've received from people who know and love you?"

"But Mom, you said I can't have my gifts till after the ceremony, so how will I know what to say?"

Dad took you to Saturday services forty-five times during the year leading up to your becoming Bar Mitzvah. He loved you and figured that the more familiar you were with your surroundings, the more comfortable you'd be "day of." Getting you to go with him each week took some of Dad's best negotiating skills, but he was as stubborn as you. In the end, he got you to go. You earned a trip to Aviation World for every four services you attended. In those pre-9/11 days, it was free to climb the stairs to the store's roof and watch the planes fly over as they came to land at Pearson Airport.

Dad is still a by-the-book kind of guy and continues to live by the rules. I was always a bit more flexible about expectations and so his standards for himself and you guys often used to drive me nuts. Thinking about it now, I realize it was a good thing because he taught you and Jonathan where the wall was, and that the wall didn't move when pushed. Because of that, you could rely on it to be there when you needed it. You wanted to wear your beloved T-shirt and sweatpants to shul, but Dad insisted you dress in a proper shirt, defined as one with buttons and a collar, and pants with a belt. In exchange for agreeing to a wardrobe modification, you lobbied to be able to bring an item from one of your collections with you to shul. Dad talked you down from a model airplane to your Toronto Transit (TTC) Metropass.

Each week at services, the rabbi and head usher, Mr. Levy, gave you a warm welcome. Mr. Levy always saved you an aisle seat so you could come and go without disturbing other worshippers. When he found out you were an Air Cadet and loved planes, he gave you the regimental RCAF flag from his World War II squadron. That flag still covers the middle window in your bedroom.

The week before your February 22 Bar Mitzvah, you caught a bad cold, and so the Friday night before, I sat by your bed handing you tissues and giving you a pep talk. Never mind that you had memorized the Hebrew verses from your portion in one week— memory was one of your greatest strengths. My worry was not about your portion but about your presentation. You were very unpredictable when you got anxious. I tried to cover up my own anxiety about all the "what if he…panics and leaves? Has to go to the bathroom and leaves? Draws a blank and stays? Giggles? Wipes his nose, or worse?" I was haunted by a recurring image of you in your new suit, shirt, and tie, putting your finger in your nose or wiping it on your sleeve or simply walking out of the service. I thought of all the school plays and concerts where you were placed in the back row to avoid drawing attention if you turned your back on the audience. And then I recalled the year that you decided to leave during one song and stepped off the top riser at the very back, crashing onto the floor behind the stands, breaking your collarbone and halting the entire performance. This drew a lot more attention than if they had placed you at the far end of one of the front rows and just let you leave if you got nervous. These thoughts conspired to make my pep talk counter-productive:

"Joel, we are so proud of all your hard work and everything you've done to prepare for your Bar Mitzvah. You are going to do such a great job tomorrow."

"Mom, my nose won't stop running."

"I know, doll, just try to forget about it."

"But it's so uncomfortable, and I can't breathe."

"I'll get you some nasal spray, and maybe that'll help."

SINCE JOEL

"Can I have another tissue, please?"

"Sure, sweetheart. Here's a whole box to keep next to you."

"Can I have it with me on the bimah tomorrow?"

"Oh…I'm not sure it'd be appropriate."

"Well, I can always use my sleeve or my hand."

Beside myself at this possibility I hissed, "Joel, I need you to listen to me very carefully because I am very serious. If I see you putting hands or sleeves or fingers near your nose tomorrow when you are on the bimah, I will break every one of your fingers."

"Mom, are you kidding me?"

"I am not. I will do it, so they better not go anywhere near your nose!"

"Can I just ask you a question, Mom?"

"Yes."

"Are you saying that because you are angry or just 'cause you're more nervous than I am?"

"Both!"

Two hours prior to the start of the service, the Bar Mitzvah family meets in the rabbi's study to go over final details and have a talk. When it was our turn, he invited us in and greeted you warmly, mentioning how pleased he was to see you each week in services.

"Today is a very good day, Joel. Mazel tov to you and your family."

You saw a wrapped gift and immediately asked: "Rabbi, is that for me?"

"Yes," he said. "It is from the congregation on the occasion of your becoming a Bar Mitzvah."

"Can I open it?"

"Yes, of course."

Disregarding the card, you tore into the wrapping to reveal a large, thick book.

"This is the Torah. How come you didn't give me something more in line with my interests?"

"Joel, this isn't so much a present for today as it is a life-long gift. It comes to you with our hope that you will continue your Jewish studies and find the Torah a helpful guide to a good life."

"Joel, please thank the rabbi."

You thanked him and leafed through the Torah.

"If it's a guide, how come it doesn't have any maps in it? Most guides have maps or at least diagrams."

Dad and the rabbi smiled. I did not. He did a final review of how the morning would unfold and then asked if any of us had any questions. You said you did.

"Rabbi, since I have a very bad cold, can I keep a box of tissues with me when I read from the Torah?"

"How about if you keep some tissues in the pocket of your new suit jacket instead?"

"That'll be okay as long as I don't forget to use them,

because last night my mother told me that if I put my hand near my nose today, she will break all my fingers."

"Is...that...what...she...said?" He drew out each word and glared at me over the rims of the half-glasses he had pulled down to the tip of his nose.

"Yes. I think it's because she's nervous, but she said she was serious. So, Rabbi, what should I do if I have to blow my nose when I am reading my portion?"

"Joel, in that case, you will reach into your pocket, take out a tissue, and blow your nose. But I will let you in on a little secret—I guarantee you that once you are up on the bimah and start your reading, you'll forget you even have a nose!"

Finally, we went down to the sanctuary and took our places in the front pews. Under the seat was my "just in case bag" full of two tissue boxes, nasal spray, and an extra shirt and fresh tie for you. As the sanctuary was filling up with guests, several of your quirky friends came to the front to greet you. Alyssa got to you first. She was tall, dark-haired, beautiful, and stuttered impossibly. She had a crush on you, and when she tried to hug you, you ducked away. Then came Eve, whose angel face and demure dress completely contradicted her loud rapid-fire questions: "Why are you having your Bar Mitzvah on February 22? Today is not your real birthday."

She still calls every year to wish you happy birthday on the right day.

Andrew peered out from his thick overhung bangs and bushy eyebrows and reminded you that he hated you and was only there because his parents forced him to come. Your classmate Jordanna's birthmark moved across her cheek when she smiled, wished you mazel tov, and told you when you're near the Torah you shouldn't chew your nails or pull at your socks and eat the threads the way you do at school.

The service began, and I tried desperately to follow along instead of marking time by counting the number of times various Hebrew letters appeared on any given page, or irreverently questioning each "blessed be he" phrase in the prayer book. I spent every ounce of energy I had willing you to sit still and behave appropriately, and nervously awaited the beginning of the Torah reading.

Exceedingly aware of the time ticking down, I was still stunned to attention when the rabbi said, "We ask the congregation to turn to page 272 as we call to the Torah our Bar Mitzvah—Joel David Schwartz, Yisroel David, ben Leipa Fishel v'Yehudit." I loved your Hebrew name because it honored Zaidy's and Pop-Pop's fathers, but I thought Dad's and my own Hebrew names sounded funny when they were read aloud. Dad's name made me think of a giant rabbit and a fish, and Yehudit sounded like someone sneezed or cleared his throat.

You heard your name, stood up, and walked forward. Almost at the top of the steps, you paused, turned around, grinned, and shot Zaidy and Pop-Pop a double thumbs up. They enthusiastically raised their arms high and signaled two thumbs up back to you. What a relief they never had to know you died. My nails were dug deep into my palms. I tried to hold my breath till you finished your portion—the way I used to do when walking under a bridge, convinced that if I made it to the other side in one breath, no pigeons would shit on me. Your uninhibited sigh of relief when you finished reading brought smiles and chuckles from the congregation. Able to breathe again, I unclenched my fists and saw tiny red half-moon shapes etched into my palms.

The gift metaphor in your portion may have gotten lost in translation, and your Bar Mitzvah speech focused entirely on the concrete, but every word you wrote was entirely you. Even though you died not knowing how to tie your shoes—according to Jewish tradition, you had become a man.

GETTING SCHOOLED

COMMON KNOWLEDGE says you can't fit a square peg into a round hole, but God knows I tried. I tirelessly filed and scraped at your square edges, and I chiseled away at the circumference of society's boundaries, desperate to fit you in. I became your ambassador. I loved you, explained you, advocated, and intervened for you. I cleaned up after you, supported you when you stumbled, comforted you when cruel bullies taunted, fooled, and pummeled you, and I hauled you to your feet when you fell down. Most importantly, though, I learned to stand aside and cheer for you as you struggled forward.

When other parents seemed to be pre-registering their toddlers for Ivy League schools, we stood in line to get you into Play and Learn, a preschool that mixed abled and disabled kids in the belief that they could all learn from each other. On the first day, you insisted on wearing your TTC streetcar T-shirt and one red and one blue sneaker. One father saw your shoes and asked if you had another pair just like them at home. "Mommy," you pulled at my hand, "how does that man know I have another pair of these shoes?"

Inside, one of the teachers greeted us warmly, gave you a name tag, and introduced you to a pretty little girl named Sibhon. She had on a pink, floral-printed, sleeveless dress and was as chatty as you were silent. Where her arms would have been, there were small knobs that looked like wing buds. Within minutes, Sibhon engaged you in gathering playthings for the two of you. Over time, she taught you how to take turns, be aware of other children, and help them with what they needed.

Play and Learn was a gift, and four years later, we lined up to get Jonathan in.

As a kid, I loved and hated my September 3 birthday. I loved getting presents but was always anxious about starting a new school year. That feeling never fully left me and became more pronounced when I had to negotiate the education system on behalf of a special needs child. When it came time for kindergarten, Bubbie and Zaidy hoped we would enroll you in a Jewish day school. I had an inkling that wouldn't work, but we agreed to apply. Some Jewish parents seem to assume that being "people of the book" guarantees having children who will be gifted. You were already reading and spelling early on, but your spatial and social disconnects conspired against any sense of normalcy, let alone genius.

The day school application was based on ten pages of five-point scales on which parents were asked to rate their five-year-old candidate on every intellectual, behavioral, emotional, and personality characteristic possible. The only question we found easy to answer was the one that asked what synagogue we belonged to. The questionnaire made us realize that while half of your brain worked like a rocket scientist, the other half didn't. There were many questions on which we couldn't even begin to rate you, so we left them blank. But in order to provide a full picture of you, your Play and Learn teacher prepared a thorough anecdotal summary of your strengths and weaknesses, which we submitted with our application.

The admissions administrator called to say that the school appreciated the written summary but could not process the application without the completed scaling questionnaire. When we explained that the questionnaire wouldn't provide a good sense of you, the administrator repeated the policy. Bubbie and Zaidy completely understood when we told them we were uncomfortable putting you in a round-hole school that didn't know anything about square pegs.

Instead, you started kindergarten at the local school, one block down the street from our house. I made myself indispensable on the Home and School Association and learned to beg, cajole, and grovel well enough to access the services that you needed. My approach to educators was always: "How can I help you help Joel?" While many teachers were truly professional and eager to have you, several made it very clear that they saw you as a burden to be shifted or a scapegoat to be blamed. I really don't know how much of it affected you, but I learned to rely on my good sense of humor and that old saw about getting more bees with honey than with vinegar. But my insides ached all the time.

Since it was unstructured time, recess, at best, saw you roaming around alone in the playground. At worst, it saw you being teased or tormented for wanting to play: "Sorry, Joel, early joiners only." You were never early. Laughter often eclipsed kindness, and the only way you were allowed to play tag was to always be "it." Every day brought new challenges, some creative solutions, small victories, setbacks, and hurt.

Each new school year I met with teachers and staff to explain Joel to them and share our strategies. Some were very grateful for our insights and input, but many seemed overwhelmed and threatened, seeing you as meaning additional work. We never told anyone it would be easy, but we always promised and made good on our availability and support.

In the best-case scenarios were the teachers who instinctively figured out ways to make use of your strengths to draw other children to you and thus have you be included organically. Your amazing verbal and spelling skills were seized upon by Mrs. Nicholls who christened you the "class dictionary" and go-to source for all things spelling and word decoding.

Worst-case situations were those where the teacher was convinced that you were malingering and could certainly perform a required task if you would just "try harder." At one conference with an art teacher who insisted that you could indeed draw the mirror image of a face, I resorted to taking a yard stick and holding it about four feet off the ground, challenging her to jump over it from a standing start. When she told me she couldn't possibly do that, I nicely suggested that perhaps she wasn't trying hard enough. That's when she "got it" and prepared some different art assignments for you, based on your insatiable interest in trains and buses.

As many times as we invited other children to play at our house, you were only asked to visit other playmates' homes five or six times. On one visit, the mother brought you home early and told me there was no point in your staying because you were more interested in her VW Beetle than in playing with her son. Too bad she never saw Walt Disney's *Herbie the Love Bug*. If she had, she could have told you Herbie wanted you to play with her little boy, and you would have done it in a minute.

Eventually we found a small private school designed to deliver the regular curriculum in ways crafted to meet each student's special needs. The strategy was simple—always use the pupil's strengths to address his/ her weaknesses. The teachers were dedicated, creative, and relentless. Even though you insisted Moby Dick was just a whale, wonderful Mrs. Weatherhead was finally able to convince you that *Animal Farm* was more than just a simple barnyard tale. You told us you liked the horses but not Napolean the pig.

Your quirks, pronounced interests, and inability to decipher social signals landed you in high school with a target on your back. Eagle-eyed bullies, many of whom were far from perfect themselves, were thrilled to have you. Mostly, you tried your best to ignore them, but they were ruthless taunters, driven by their own insecurities. You were as clumsy as you were large, and you rarely fought back. First of all, we had taught you that hitting was unacceptable, and secondly, you couldn't land a punch if you tried. You had no aim, and you always stamped your foot before you threw your arm. At one point, we thought humor might diffuse the attacks, so we practiced "quick comebacks." You once asked a boy who swore at you whether he "ate with that dirty mouth." That boy caught you, shoved your face into the earth, and gave you the dirty mouth. Whenever you tried to run, they caught you and punished you with barbed words and heavy fists. Early on, Dad and I had tried to reassure you that being different was fine. Well, kiddo, we were wrong. Turns out, being different is not fine at all.

"Mom, I'm home from school and I'm starved. Can I have some cookies?"

"Of course, but just tell me how was your day?"

"Better than usual since they expelled Carlos."

"What? Did they actually make him leave for good?"

"Yup. A week after he beat me up in the washroom, he punched another kid in the head and knocked him unconscious, and school called the cops. That kid's parents pressed charges, and Mr. Victor expelled Carlos."

"Did the police come into school?"

"Uh-huh. And they wanted to interview me about what Carlos did to me in the bathroom."

"Did you tell them everything?"

"I said he duct taped my hands together and punched me in the head and said I was Olympic in a special way. I told them I didn't understand that, but I could tell it wasn't nice. They asked me if Carlos did anything else, but I said I was too embarrassed to show them where else he punched me."

"Oh my God, Joel, that must have been so upsetting to talk about."

"Nowhere near as bad as trying to hide from him every day. Anyway, the cops thanked me and said I was brave to tell them. And Mom, they let me hold their police scanner for a bit. Carlos is finally gone now, so school will be better."

"That really must be a huge relief. Do you have any homework?"

"Just a philosophy assignment for Mr. Mavriganis that's due tomorrow. Did you move the cookie tin? I'm really hungry."

"I put it in a different spot so you wouldn't finish them all. Tell me about your assignment, and I'll get you some cookies."

"Mr. Mav wants us to think like a philosopher and tell in our own words what Aristotle meant when he said you can never step in the same river twice."

"What do you think that means?"

"I'm not sure…. If Jonathan and I swim in the same lake over and over each summer, why can't someone step in the same river twice?"

"Try to think about what happens when you step in a river and imagine what the philosopher is trying to say."

"Maybe it's that if I'm gonna step in a river, I would take off my socks and shoes, and my feet would be dirty from the riverbank when I walk in. And maybe that dirt from my toes would wash off into the river water."

"And what would that mean?"

"I'd have clean feet!"

"Very funny. But what about the river?"

"It would have all my foot and toe dirt in it. So it's like it's the same river, but once I step in it, I make it different. Mom, can I please have my cookies?"

"For sure."

"Mom?"

"Yes."

"Do you think all those times Jonathan and I peed in the lake means no one can ever swim in that same lake twice?"

Along with Mr. Mav, Mrs. Sallay, and Mr. Johnson were the guardian angels who worked tirelessly to create as positive a high-school experience as possible for you; and they even made it look easy. Do you remember all those times Mr. Johnson invited you to sit with him in the cafeteria at lunch? And how Mrs. Sally always seemed to know what teacher would be best for you? They knew how to adjust expectations without ever lowering them; and for that I will always be grateful.

THE ROUTINE

AFTER HIGH SCHOOL, your collections expanded to include airplane safety cards, walkie-talkies, scanners, news articles about disasters, and hurt feelings as the result of many social mistakes. But you were punctual, reliable, and guided by an internal GPS; and you finally earned a position with a public transit-based courier service called A-Way Express. A-Way was a social purpose enterprise that understood the value and importance of providing meaningful employment for square pegs.

Customers could set their clocks by you, and you never missed a deadline. You were provided a uniform, courier bag, two-way radio, and a sense of purpose. You took your responsibilities seriously and were truly professional in an industry that often was not. Admitting you weren't quite ready to move out, you continued to live with us.

Each afternoon when your A-Way shift ended, you'd TTC home, burst into the house, shout: "Mom, I'm home," and head upstairs. You'd peel off your jeans, remove your socks, underwear, and T-shirt, then ball them together, toss them into the laundry hamper, and from the kitchen, I could hear you call out, "Two points." You always folded a pair of fresh new jeans over the desk chair so that two thirds of each leg hung down, and you placed a clean sock in each L.L. Bean Comfort Moc. Then, standing naked, you'd pile a fresh version of the rest of the next day's outfit on top of the jeans so that the item at the top was the first one to be put on in the morning. With this layer-cake of clothing complete, you'd duck into the shower, hose yourself off, and towel dry. Next, you'd jump into the only pajama bottoms you would wear—the flannel ones with the John Deere logo that you called "jammy botts." On top, you wore a ratty black-fleece thing that may have, at one time, been a sweatshirt.

At 5:45 each evening, I'd call you to the table and keep you company while you scarfed down dinner. It never varied: two slices of meatloaf (not always completely thawed), a handful of carrots (because I said so), and a baked potato. Everything swam in ketchup. We had tried mightily to create the dinner scene we imagined other families enjoyed—the one where everyone sits around a nicely set table, shares a good meal, and discusses the day's goings on. But it never seemed to happen for us. You always came home from work at five, starving. Jonathan always had a hockey game, and Dad and I always seemed to have evening meetings to attend. I purposely tried not to pry or ask you too many questions while you were eating, and I think you were relieved at not having to talk. Maybe it made it easier for you to gather yourself for the nightly call to your girlfriend, Diana. "Mom," you'd say when you were finished eating, "I'm going to my room to call Diana." Upstairs, your voice was so loud that I could hear you rehash your day, ask about hers, and then try to make plans to get together.

I never really expected that you would ever have a girlfriend in any sense of the word. Intimate relationships are so fraught with nuance—and you could barely negotiate a straight forward conversation—that I got quite comfortable cushioning myself with the idea that at least you and "we" would be spared having to work our way through romance. The day you came home and told me about Diana that cushion began to fray.

"Mom—I met this girl and she likes me."

"JoJo what makes you think so?"

"She told me. She said out loud she likes me and she wants to go on a date with me."

About a week later, when you came back from the date, I asked how it went.

"It was fine. She took me to visit Andrew."

"Who is Andrew, and where did you meet him?"

"Mom, he has a tiny headstone in a special part of the cemetery because he only lived for a week. The doctor told Diana that something was wrong, and Andrew was a 'bad baby' and couldn't live…. She told me she's okay now and says she's over it 'cause it happened when she was fourteen, and she's older now."

I think I mumbled something about what a sad thing had happened and that losing a child must be an awful experience.

You told me you understood how she got pregnant, but you said you weren't sure why she got pregnant.

When your nightly call with Diana went well, you were relaxed. You'd come and lounge around in the family room and tell me all the things you and Diana had planned. But more often than not, there were misunderstandings, high drama, and an abruptly ended conversation, followed by your wailing, "She hung up on me again!" Then you would have a meltdown, and in a cyclone of self-destructive disappointment you would stomp around the house, chew your nails, throw your phone, pig out on cookies, and, between belches, try fruitlessly to reach her over and over. I tried to take cover till the winds died down. Finally spent, you'd go to your room, monitor your police scanner, set the alarm to wake up for work, show your teeth a toothbrush, and get into bed.

TAURUS AND THE MANATEE

THE FIRST TIME I saw Diana I thought of an albino manatee—one of the large, hulking creatures that galumph along in the Florida intercoastal waters—so unattractive as to appeal. Like these marine giants, Diana had long, slender fingers and toes that seemed to meld one into the next and taper so that her hands and feet appeared to be flippers. Her face was pale, white, and flat...somewhere between an egg and a full moon. She wore her sparse blonde hair in braided cornrows finished off with beads, and her pink scalp looked angry in between the rows.

During adolescence, you had morphed from a sprite-like stickman into a tree trunk with massive branches. Your facial features broadened along with the metamorphosis. Your eyebrows grew to meet each other, and you had a heavy beard. Not the best or most careful of shavers, your jaw and neck were often clotted with StipTik-cauterized cuts. You were graceless but purposeful and clumsy but determined—truly the Taurus of your zodiac sign.

You and Diana met at a job readiness program for people with "barriers to employment." You were there to improve your social skills, and she was learning to cook. You were living in our basement, and social services had just removed Diana from her father's home and placed her in a women's shelter. When I asked about that, you said it had to do with her father keeping the fridge door locked and something called "domestic servitude." My mind went to very bad places. In addition to seeing each other at the job prep program, you visited Diana at the shelter every night. Many residents were wary of men, but they and the staff came to know and trust you; and you earned the privilege of waiting in the lobby when you came to pick Diana up.

Given all the challenges you and Diana faced, your acne and her psoriasis seemed insults added to injury. But miraculously you were each blind to the other's logo of unwanted distinction. I imagined the pair of you as *American Gothic* gone wrong, and wondered how other people felt when they saw you two walking hand in hand. Did they stare? Did they avert their gaze? Maybe some stifled laughter, but perhaps some clucked to each other and smiled gently. Somehow, in an ungainly dance, you and Diana filled each other's gaps. She shopped, hoarded, ate, called everyone she knew, and played Special Olympics bowling and baseball. You visited bus, subway, and train stations, drove her to games and practices and malls, and bought her Tim's Iced Capps, phone cards, and fast food. When you brought her to our house, you said she was trying very hard to lose weight and always encouraged us to compliment her on how much thinner she looked. We smiled and said how happy we were for her; but, of course, she never lost an ounce. And there was the time you told us how proud you were of Diana when she found a wallet on the TTC. She told us she "kept the money because she needed it," but she turned in the wallet and cards "'cause I am an honest person."

I remember one night you thundered into the house after midnight from an evening with Diana. I was in the kitchen cleaning up dishes from dinner, and you hollered, "Mom...guess what?"

I turned around to see you pumping your fist into the air and yelling, "I got lucky!"

I didn't know whether to laugh or cry; but before

I could say or do anything you lowered your voice to a hoarse, conspiratorial whisper.

"But don't worry, Mom, we used a condom."

For a moment, it brought me back to the time you came home from an elementary school class in sex ed and told me you learned that "ovaries are like the storage cupboards for your eggs," and that you had practiced putting a condom on a broomstick handle.

Even though I never thought dating and girl-friends would make it into the lexicon of your life, and that Diana was not the daughter-in-law of my dreams, I convinced myself to accept her simply because she was someone who seemed to make you happy. I also recognized that no matter how odd the couple, relationships were part of "being normal." In our efforts to make her feel welcome, Dad and I ended up bending over backward to avoid dwelling on her misfortunes and to help her out of tough situations. We came to learn, along with you, that a happy Diana meant a happy Joel. But keeping Diana happy proved to be a long game.

One evening you called from a police station in a panic to say that Diana was in jail because she had "ignored her bench warrant," whatever that meant. Well, it meant she had been charged with assaulting someone on a streetcar and was supposed to be fulfilling her "diversion sentencing" by checking in with the court on a regular basis, and that she had failed to do so and was now under arrest! This was not a book we had ever read, but you were hysterical and insisted that we "come down here right now and get her out of jail." I made Daddy go to help, and I don't know what he managed to say or do, and he doesn't even recall, but she was released and given "one more chance."

By the time you met Diana, she had very little contact with her own parents and family, and even less money. When the winter came and I saw her one tattered, thin jacket, I offered to buy her a new one. At the store, she reminded me that she also needed a hat and gloves and scarf and boots. Could I say no? Not for these or any of the other necessities she was without. I took her to a sporting goods store and headed to the rack of larger sized women's jackets, but not even the XXXL would zip closed over her stomach and chest. She was hoping for purple and pink, but it soon became clear that we needed to find the menswear section, where she was resigned to green, navy blue, or gray. Several salespeople hung around the edges of the displays, but none seemed at all interested in getting involved. I could almost feel their eyes crawling over her heft, but she seemed unaware. In the end, we found a green jacket with beige piping—and she was able to zip it completely from bottom to top. I was glad it had a hood. She said she still wanted a pink or purple hat "to go with it."

In Diana we inherited a daughter we didn't want but couldn't dismiss. She had moved from the shelter to a small single room in public housing, so our basement furnace room became the repository for garbage bags full of clothing she had collected from Goodwill, along with possessions she was allowed to remove from her father's house. It began to feel like she was here even when she wasn't, and she was here a lot. I'd see her seated at your desk, trolling your computer for Back Street Boys' song lyrics while you'd lie on your bed reading street car manuals. I used to wish you and she would hang out at her place, until one day I went there to drop off some "healthy food" for her. The building was a former hotel, and her narrow room consisted of space for a bed and dresser and small closest. There was no actual kitchen, but instead, a microwave, hot plate, and a bar fridge under a table at the entrance. An afterthought of a bathroom was off to the side of the main door. It was a ridiculously impossible place to call home, but it was hers. A neat person may have been able to create a livable setting, but what I saw was a disaster. The bed was piled high with dirty clothing and newspapers that she was "saving for you," and the floor was strewn with sheets and more filthy unidentifiable objects. I picked my way to the "kitchen," and when I opened the fridge to put in some fresh vegetables, I drew back from the smell. Every item stuffed in it was months beyond any best before date. I helped her throw out spoiled food and inserted newer options. Diana told me the place was hard to keep clean, and each time tenants got notices about fumigation for pests and rodents, she'd bring more things to our house because she "really didn't want to get bed bugs."

Because she meant so much to you, we often included Diana at family dinners and holiday celebrations. She wanted to put her cooking skills to good use and once asked if she could prepare homemade macaroni and cheese for one of our Friday night Shabbat dinners. These meals were usually meat-based, so normally did not include any dishes made with milk products in order to abide by the rules of kashruth. Dad and I decided to make an exception in order to give Diana an opportunity to contribute and feel appreciated when Jonathan was coming in from Montreal for the weekend, and our cousins were also joining for dinner. She gave me a list of ingredients to purchase, which I did, and a recipe that she would follow when she arrived at our house that Friday afternoon. The afternoon came and went, and in the early evening she called to ask if I'd boiled the macaroni, mixed the cheeses together, and put it all in the casserole dish so she could "put it in the oven" and have it ready for when we were going to eat. When she failed to show up by seven that evening, I hustled the mixture into the oven at 400 degrees. There it sat, one shelf above my perfect brisket. You kept calling and calling her to no avail, and eventually we all gathered around the table and said the blessing over the bread and wine and candles. When Diana finally did show up, she asked when she could serve the macaroni and cheese that she "had made for us for dinner."

Jonathan, never her fan, caught my eye and rolled his eyes at this obvious untruth. He was convinced she was taking complete advantage of you and never missed an opportunity from home or afar to bring her faults to the fore.

When you found out about Diana's "new friend," Mike, you fumed and stamped around the house loudly asking, "Why is she doing this to me? Why does she spend time with him?" In an effort to sort things out, you brought Diana over to our house, and we listened to her explain to you that Mike had dated her mother but was her own friend now, and that you shouldn't worry because, "He always sleeps on the floor when he stays over at my place." She actually made it sound so totally logical that another man who *had dated her mother* was sleeping over in her room that we joined her in telling you not to worry.

Over time, Diana's issues and crises cast long shadows. While he never spoke sharply to her, Jonathan's musings about her motivations were troublingly true. We told him that we totally understood his perspective, but that to be fair, we all needed to consider that she had learned to be manipulative in order to survive, rather than in order to be hurtful. We also reminded him that in spite of all the trouble, she often made you happy. Taking all this into consideration, he once invited the two of you to visit him at McGill. You were thrilled that he included you in his university life, and that he was willing to have Diana join in. After the visit, Jonathan phoned to tell us that at dinner one evening at Baton Rouge, you accidently bumped into another diner's wine, and when it spilled you apologized and pulled out your wallet and offered to pay the cleaning bill. The man declined, and Jonathan told you how proud of you he was, and then told us how upset he was when Diana claimed she was the one who told you to offer to pay. After you died, Jonathan made it very clear to Dad and me that he would kill Diana if she showed her face at your funeral. A day or two after you died, she actually did call our house to say she'd heard what happened and just wanted us to know that she felt it would be too difficult for her to come to the funeral. She said your death was "very, very hard on her." I ended the call telling her I understood. Several years later, I spotted her out front of the Special Olympics bowling location. I was driving your Jetta, and for a moment I think she may have noticed the car and the license. When the light changed, I sped off.

MAGICAL ISLAND

TWO MONTHS AFTER your death, I was in un-
charted territory, having never lived without you longer
than the span of your summers away at camp. With
time, I now understand and can even accept that you
are gone. What I still don't get is that you are gone
because you are dead. Gone—yes. Dead—how is that
possible? Maybe it's that gone contains the possibility
of return, but dead does not.

When you were very young and we didn't yet
know how different you were, we thought to send you
to a children's day camp that many neighbors recom-
mended. Dad and I had each loved summer camp, and
when we signed you up and told you all about the kids
you'd meet and activities you'd get to do, you asked

about the activity schedule and whether Thomas the Tank Engine could come with you to camp.

Your thin stem of a neck held your head of unruly curls, a dandelion bobbing out of a fresh white T-shirt, while your spindly legs poked out below the cuffs of blue shorts and took their sweet time getting you to the car. No one let me in on the carpool scene, so I drove to camp on that first day. You weren't too eager to leave me, but when your unit head came to the office to pick you up and go to where the campers were gathering, you took his hand and went along. He was very tall, and when the two of you walked off, it looked like you were his teddy bear. By the time I got back to our house, there was a message from camp saying that you were having a hard time staying with your group and following instructions, and wondering if I had any suggestions. I asked them to be patient because new situations were hard for you.

Day one of week two, you didn't want to go to camp. You said you didn't like it when your counselor put you "in handcuffs." I didn't understand what you meant, and when you showed me what he did to you when you wandered off, I called the camp and asked for a meeting. Your counselor was relieved of his duties when he admitted that his idea of "managing" you was to bungee-cord your wrists together, tie you to a tree,

and threaten what would happen if you told anyone
about it. You never did tell on him. You only said you
didn't want to go to camp because you didn't like wearing handcuffs.

There was so much I didn't know that I just accepted the camp's decision to not keep you as a camper
anymore. It felt as if I had been given back a damaged item that didn't fit in a display case of perfection.
Rather than put you where you weren't wanted, I plot-
ted revenge and decided to out-camp camp. Wishing
to accomplish this while preserving my sanity led me
to an ingenious solution. Rather than stay home listening to you rattle on about trains, why not pack picnic
lunches and go to see trains in action? Turns out that
Toronto has hundreds of rail-oriented observation
posts, and many people who visit them. Your favorite
was when we would plant ourselves on the Hillsdale
bridge over the Davisville TTC tracks and wait for
subway trains to pass under us. We waved at oncom-
ing engineers, and many would blow their horns and
wave back to us. It was wonderful to see you get so
excited, a windup toy jumping and turning in circles
all at once. Often, the only way to get you back in the
car to go home was with a bribe for a chocolate-chip
cookie-dough Dairy Queen. A time-limited offer with
a ten-minute expiry.

Eventually, we did find a day camp run by people who understood your differences. Your favorite activity was the bus ride to and from the campsite. Each bus had a counselor, and yours chose you to be her special assistant to welcome each camper onto the bus. That meant you had to interact directly with other kids and got to sit right behind the driver—where you wanted to be and where the bus counselor could always see you. Three birds with one stone. You knew every camper and every driver's name, the detailed specs of all the vehicles, every route they traveled, and the contact information for the bus company. You even charmed your way into being the keeper of bus schedules and the one who called out the buses at boarding time; and you earned yourself a FirstTran bus mug and T-shirt. Best of all, you also learned to canoe, swim, and make some craft pieces. I still have the necklace you made for me from a rock wrapped in thin wire and strung on a leather thong.

One day early on in the camp session, I asked you to tell me about the kids in your bunk, and you told me that there was a boy in your cabin who wasn't from Canada.

"JoJo, what's the boy's name?"

"Joshua."

"How do you know he isn't from Canada?"

"He doesn't speak English."

"Do you know where he's from?"

"Nope."

The next week I asked, "Is the boy learning any English words?"

"I don't think so."

"Have you tried to teach him some? You know so many words, maybe you could help him."

"Mom, he doesn't like to talk."

"Oh, I see. Do you think he is shy?"

"Maybe. He also forgets to wipe his mouth."

"What do you mean?"

"Well, lots of times there is this stuff that spills out."

"What kind of stuff?"

"I don't know but it looks yucky…like nose stuff but in his mouth."

"Do the counselors know?"

"Yeah, and they remind him to wipe it off and sometimes help him when it gets really bad."

"What are his favorite activities?"

I think he likes arts and crafts, but it's hard for him to make things."

"How come?"

"Because he holds one of his hands in a funny way…like it's stuck in an upside-down letter C. Mom, could I please have some cookies now?"

"Sure, doll. Do people help Joshua?"

"Yes, Mom. We all take turns pushing his wheelchair when we go to activities."

۹۰

When it came time for you to try sleepaway camp, a magical place called John Island turned out to be a distant but wonderful ally. A social worker suggested we contact the Sudbury YMCA because their Camp John Island was very inclusive and not only talked the talk but also knew how to walk the walk. Who could have guessed that Sudbury would steal all of our hearts?

The director invited us to come up for a visit before camp started, and you loved the idea because Sudbury was one of the stops on your favorite train, The Canadian. Our five-hour drive paralleled much of the CN track line, and you were mesmerized—calling out every station from Washago to Sudbury Junction. The area really does look like the moonscape that drew NASA to train astronauts on that terrain. We learned that "Sudbury Rocks," in more ways than one.

In our visit with the director, we were completely upfront about your differences. He nodded and said he didn't really see any of your issues as being a problem for anyone at camp. He showed us the camp manual where the policies were laid out on one page for parents and on the opposite page for kids. It was brilliant. It informed parents that there was an active wildlife community at the camp and that sending packages of treats would likely attract animals. The kids' version said that if they got treats, they could expect to be sharing their beds with Rocky Raccoon and his buddies! In explaining inclusion, the manual told parents that children of many different backgrounds would be attending camp and that everyone was welcome. The kids' page reminded campers that some children are good at sports, some are good at music, some are good at art, and that everyone is good at something.

At the end of the visit, the director asked if you had any questions. Dad and I were astonished to hear you ask: "If this is a YMCA camp and I am a J...is that going to be a problem?" The director didn't miss a beat. He said, "Joel, at this camp you are welcome no matter what letter you are."

Your camp duffle bags included your own PFD (personal flotation device). While the Sudbury Y was downtown, Camp John Island itself lay in the North Channel of Lake Huron and could only be accessed by boat. The crossing went to and from a desolate dock on land owned by the Serpent River Nation just outside the small town of Spanish. You told us that before it was a campsite, John Island housed a logging camp and the first semi-professional baseball field in Ontario. It was rugged, wild, and windswept. Even though cabins, dining, rec halls, and out-buildings perched onshore, it was clear that humans were only there as visitors and that the whole place belonged to nature.

Camp John Island was your crucible. Its challenges and supports molded you. In that remote but welcoming place, you came to know that actions have consequences. That people who like you for who you are also expect you to behave appropriately—and that they will help you do that. That everyone has a place, and no one is just a placeholder. And that nature is in charge, and if she says it's too windy to canoe, the boats stay beached that day.

You learned how to run across the bows of water-borne kayaks in a line—piano keying. When you got tired on a long hike, the "bush doctor" picked you up, spun you around, put you down, and taught you that you could always go a little farther than you thought. You met your first girlfriend there; and courtesy of the surrounding waters and patient instructors, you became a powerful swimmer. After slamming into a tree on the zip line, you learned to always face forward. And after an extraordinary number of attempts, you made it to the top of the climbing rock and completed the ropes course. Your built-in compass made you a prized navigator on out-trips, and your self-deprecating sense of humor made you a welcome relief in tense situations.

In all, you spent seven summers at John Island, going from camper to CIT (counselor in training) to eventually working on the maintenance staff. You adored every camp dog from Comet to Rags, whose white spot on his bum made you ask if he sat in bleach as a puppy. Each winter holiday, the beautiful and decent young people from camp took turns inviting you to Sudbury, where you got to snowmobile across a frozen Ramsay Lake and head to their family "camps" in the wilderness. Dad and I still can't get over the photo Dan's father took of you and Dan, each holding an antler on the head of a moose he had downed. I despised the idea of hunting, but I loved Dan's family of hunters.

During one of your early summers at John Island, Dad and I went to spend the session changeover weekend with you in Sudbury. We arranged for the three of us to stay at the Travel Lodge. We arrived in time to pick you up when the camp bus rolled into town and then drove to the hotel. Dad dropped us off to check in and went to park and unload the car. When the automatic door slid open to allow us in, I heard myself gasp. We waded into a sea of black leather, silver chains, blue ink on naked skin, and an awful lot of hair. I saw your eyes get big, and before you could say anything, I used my best side-of-the-mouth whisper to tell you not to say a word. We waited in the check-in line sandwiched between two vested but shirtless hairy men.

You waited a few seconds and then loudly asked, "Mom, why shouldn't I say anything?"

I died as the men and others near us chuckled and said, "Lady, let the boy ask whatever he wants."

I apologized and fumbled around with saying something about not wanting to disturb them. You said, "Mom, if the guys say I can ask questions, can I?"

"Sure you can, buddy," said the one with a black bandana covering his head and a skull-and-crossbones earring dangling down. "Do you like motorcycles?"

"Yeah, I like anything with wheels, and I especially like Harley Davidsons." A few more of them came over and nodded their approval.

"How come you guys aren't wearing shirts?"

"Oh God, Joel…"

"It's okay. It's a good question. The shirts cover up our tattoos."

Of course—silly me—why else go shirtless?

"Hey pal, how'd you like to see our bikes when we're all done checking in?"

Oh, my God, they really are staying here at our hotel.

"Mom, can I go see their motorcycles later?"

"Don't worry, Ma'am, if he likes bikes, he's safe with us. Just bring him to the back parking lot, and we'll show him around." He winked, finished checking in, and high-fived you.

We checked in next and went to help Dad with the bags. When we got to our room on the third floor, you opened the curtains and, sure enough, we were overlooking the back parking lot packed full with a circle of motorcycles in every color known to man. From high up, they were jeweled charms you could hang on a bracelet, shined to perfection and set with blue sapphire, emeralds, rubies, and tourmalines. A gigantic leather-clad man with fringed chaps and a head that resembled a cue ball sat as the sentry in the middle of the circle.

You wanted to eat dinner at Pizza Hut, and when we got back to the hotel, the sun was going down.

"Mom, I want to see the bikes."

"Are you sure you aren't tired?"

Can't blame me for trying.

"No, the guys said I could visit the bikes in the parking lot."

Dad said he would take you, and I went, weak-kneed, up to our room. I snuck a look out of the window and saw the black leather giant clap you on the back and shake Dad's hand. It's not often that I think of Dad as small, but his six-foot-two frame didn't hold a candle to the bike guard. You guys all seemed to be talking and then as the biker took you from bike to bike, he gestured for Dad to leave. As he did, I grabbed the room key and raced to the stairs to scream for Dad to get back to the parking lot and stay with you. We met in the stairwell, and he insisted I calm down. He was as thoroughly convinced that you would come to no harm as I was that you would be borne away by a horde of lunatics. Dad told me the guy had said to pick you up in a half hour. Dad also reminded me that after a half hour of your questions, the man would probably be very happy to let you come back to us.

In fact, that's exactly what happened. The next morning, when we came downstairs to check out, the hotel was swarming with local police and RCMP officers. They warned everyone that there was a large contingent of Hell's Angels in Sudbury for a convention and that "everyone should exercise extreme caution when in contact with them." You started to say something, but we interrupted, thanked the police, and then drove you to the pick-up point in time to catch the camp bus back to the ferry to John Island.

All of your John Island treasures are still in your room: the JIC dining hall coffee cup, your JIC baseball

cap, the navy-blue fleece staff jacket with JOEL embroi-
dered on the chest, photos, letters, and your hard-won
NHOJ PMAC (Camp John backwards) maintenance
uniform. Once in a while, I put on the fleece jacket
and snuggle into it for just a few minutes...but not for
long because I don't want to get used to wearing it. Two
summers after you died, some of the John Islanders
traveled to Toronto for a weekend. They stopped by
our house to say hello. Knowing how much you loved
the TTC, they told us they'd spent that Saturday afternoon riding full loops of the Yonge-University subway
in your memory.

THE WASHAGO MOOSE

ON THURSDAY, July 31, I left YMCA John Island Camp for the last time that summer. It was the best one of my life. People were friendly, the camp was set on an exquisite island in the North Channel, and I was a success at every activity I tried. The last day of camp was happy and sad at the same time. I was happy to be coming home and I was sad to be leaving camp.

The actual trip home was exciting because I was getting to travel from Sudbury to Toronto on a legendary train called THE CANADIAN. Once we came ashore from camp, Dave and Fraser drove me to the Sudbury Junction train station. When we got there, we found out that The Canadian was delayed and wouldn't be in until 7 p.m. That gave us time for dinner, so Dave

and Fraser took me to McDonald's and then drove me
back to the station. At seven o'clock, I saw the lights of
the locomotive in the distance while a station attendant's voice boomed out over the P.A. system: "Arriving
on track B, train number two—The Canadian." The
closer it got, the bigger it seemed. The engine was huge
and beautiful and soon it was about to hurl down the
tracks and take me home.

I threw my duffel into the baggage car, said good-
bye and thanks to Fraser and Dave, jumped onto the
train and found my seat. We jerked backward, then
forward as the train pulled away. We traveled along,
and after night fell, I could see the Big Dipper from
my coach window. Eventually I fell asleep. I got shaken
awake when the train came to a halt. The conductor
came through the car announcing: "There is a moose
on the tracks just north of Washago Station. If we can't
move the moose, you all will be spending the night in
Washago at the hotel there." The next thing I knew, I
was off The Canadian and in the Hotel Washago. We
could see the moose and a bunch of train employees
surrounding it. The moose was in no mood to move
and wouldn't budge.

I was shown to my room, which was on the third
floor. It was quite small with plain furniture. It had
a desk, a lamp, a chair, and a bed that were not at all

modern. The walls had wallpaper with a spotted design. The window was open. I began to unpack just a pair of pyjamas and a book to read. I put the book down on the desk and looked to my right as something caught my eye. It was a white triangle with a tiny red maple leaf in a blue circle. I knew the shape and the symbols looked familiar. I picked it up and it turned out to be a small model of the Avro Arrow. Only one person I ever knew had that size perfect model of the famous Avro Arrow. That was a man named Shawn Walsh. Walsh was the captain and commanding officer of my old Air Cadet Squadron, the 180 Mosquito Squad based out of Toronto. I was an Air Cadet and plane crazy back then and Walsh used to show me his model Arrow when I got my drill steps correct at our Friday night parade meetings.

The only way for that model plane to have ended up in the Hotel Washago was if Captain Shawn Walsh had stayed in my third floor room. I decided to take the model with me back to Toronto and then plan to go to the 180 Parade Square on a Friday night. I bet I will see Capt. Walsh calling our drill commands and I will give him back his model and ask if he enjoyed his stay at the Hotel Washago. After thinking back more about Walsh and how fair he was and how he taught his cadets about flying, military style drill, discipline, and esprit de corps, I fell asleep.

The next morning, I woke up when I heard three knocks at my door. I stretched and got out of bed. I opened the door and saw a CP Rail employee standing in the doorway. He said, "The moose finally moved late last night, and our path is clear. We will be boarding in half an hour." I started to pack and then I decided I would leave an object behind that would give the next guest a clue that I had stayed in the room. In my bag, I had an extra John Island Camp T-shirt with my name sewed in the label, so I left it in the room.

I left the hotel and headed back to the train. I threw my bag into the baggage car and an attendant directed me back to my coach. I heard the humming of the big diesel engine at the front of The Canadian and knew we were finally homeward bound. When I arrived at home, I figured out a good Friday to visit Walsh at Air Cadets, and I started to wonder if somebody would actually find my T-shirt in the room and ever return it to me. It had been the best summer ever.

—by Joel Schwartz

৽

I often find myself in your room, where I sit down in different spots and reach out to pick up whatever is close at hand. Once, I opened your desk drawer and way in the back I found a copy of a story of yours called "The Washago Moose." You wrote it for a grade ten English assignment on the subject of legacies. While ASD gifted you with a talent for facts and information, it confounded your ability to comprehend concepts, symbolism, and fiction. I remember the day I got very frustrated trying to discuss the notion of a legacy with you. How come you simply couldn't process the idea of leaving something behind for others? When I finally cornered you with that question in concrete terms, you said you had an idea. That's when you wrote "The Washago Moose."

We have come a long way since then, but not anywhere near to where I am comfortable cleaning out your room. It feels like anything I part with will be just one more piece of you gone. And like you, once it's gone, it's gone for good. In the end, I suppose none of the items matter; and I won't ever really lose you until I die too. Still, the thought of tossing out or giving away any of your planes, trains, buses, or your collection of airline safety cards and disaster photos seems like a slight to all the energy you put into gathering them.

Anything with your name on it is here to stay. You can rest assured your John Island Camp staff jacket and your Holy Blossom caretaker shirt and your Air Cadet wings are not going anywhere. I think as long as I can remind myself of your face and voice and laugh and smell, you are with me in some way.

FAMILY ROOM

DAD AND I bought our house in 1980 and poured all our earnings into it. Lollie and Pop-Pop came from Philly to see it, and when Zaidy picked them up from the airport and drove them to the house, Lollie refused to leave the car. "I can see from here that it looks just like Aunt Evie's tiny little place in Mt. Airy. Norman," she hissed at Pop-Pop, "I can't believe they spent so much money to live on a dead-end street in a house that has a front stoop." And with that, she ordered Zaidy to "please drive on." Lollie was right about many things, but our house turned out to be the smartest move Dad and I ever made.

Three years later, when we knew we were having a family, we decided to add a family room. Neighbors teased that the perimeter of the house was expanding along with my belly. The contractor was Dutch and told us he "refused to add boxes to houses." Instead, he produced a pentagonal addition that was as unique as it was difficult to furnish. Our new room's longest wall had no windows, three other walls had window banks, and the fifth wall housed a French glass door that opened to the deck. But for a large, leafy green plant, the room sat empty for quite some time. With so much light and so many sight lines into the yard, it was hard to tell whether the plant was inside or outside. When we finally found a perfect marble coffee table with a four-foot by four-foot top, it spoke to us and came home to anchor the new room. Its large surface became the steady center of movie nights, birthday parties, holidays, sleepovers, and family get-togethers. You and Jonathan hid beneath it and presented puppet shows. We ate pizza on it, argued across it, slid mini-pucks end to end, and stained it with plenty of good times.

One January day, I came home from work and found you in the family room—a six-foot, two-hundred-and-fifty-pound pillar of stone rooted to the floor in front of our marble coffee table. The lines in your forehead were twisted into ruts, and your hands held each other in a death grip. Knowing something was terribly wrong, I got distracted for a minute thinking that you looked like your old André the Giant wrestling figure and half expected to hear Vince McMahon announce, "Here he is, impervious to pain…André the Giant… looking bigger than I've ever seen him look!" For years you used to imitate that announcement and crack us up.

I took a chance. "Hi, Joel. How was your day?"

You lurched for the phone, and a strange voice burst out of your mouth: "I'll show you how my fucking day was. I'M DIALING 9-1-1 RIGHT NOW!" You were on the verge, but I was hoping you were crying wolf.

"Please, JoJo, you know you should save 9-1-1 for real emergencies."

De-escalation had trumped hysteria in the past, so my default tone was slow and steady.

I know that living just next to normal has been an enormous challenge for you; and I don't know how you have done it for your whole life. I know that watching normal, wanting it, and trying but never achieving it has taken a toll. Your bounce-back quotient has been extraordinary. But it wasn't this time.

You stopped mid-dial and shrieked, "Diana dumped me again, and this time she says she means it. She said she never wants to see me again, and no matter how many times I call her, she won't pick up her phone. What will I do now?"

The agony of permanence landed on my little boy who once told his father, "There's no such thing as the wrong bus, Daddy; buses can't be wrong."

Another meltdown, courtesy of a life of misunderstanding. The Vaseline-smeared glasses of Asperger's clouded your perception, leaving you desperate to live in our world, but only in your own rigid, repetitive way.

Before I could speak, you hoisted and somehow hurled the marble tabletop across the family room. For a split second, it seemed weightless, until it thundered down, clattering into hundreds of miniature pieces. Roman ruins cast across the hardwood floor.

"There," you heaved. "Broken, just like my whole fucking life."

At that moment, I was terrified and froze as Piper yelped and bolted for cover.

You grabbed the phone again and this time stabbed out 9-1-1 in my face. The connection was almost immediate.

"This is a domestic emergency," you bellowed. "I'm calling in a domestic emergency.... No, no one is hurt yet, but I just smashed a marble table and really scared my mom and the dog. Here with me? Just me, her, and the dog. Yes, my name is Joel Schwartz. Yes, that's our address. You have to come soon."

You hung up and instantly looked relieved that it was done.

I found the dog and, dragging him with me, backed away, edged my way upstairs to the bedroom and closed the door. You'd lashed out before, but never like this. The surreal notion that you might actually hurt me snuck into my head and settled painfully.

You followed me upstairs and begged me to open the bedroom door.

"Mom, what will happen now? I'm so sorry, and I promise I won't ever do this again. I can help clean up the mess right now.... Please don't tell Dad." A guilty puppy whimpering for forgiveness.

I have been your ambassador for twenty-five years. I've explained you, cleared paths, broken ice, pleaded for services, cheered you on, and picked up the pieces each time you crashed. But 9-1-1 was an indelible call, and I couldn't protect you anymore.

The dog barked, and from the bedroom window I could see that a police car had already arrived and parked across from our house. Two officers strode gingerly up our driveway. One was tall, dark, and slim; and the other, short, stocky, and pale. It seemed like it took this oddly mismatched pair only seconds to get to our house.

You were at the front door as soon as they knocked. I crept out of the bedroom and worked my way down onto the landing. I was numb. My mind was stuck, and I think my heart was actually broken. You yanked open the door, announced that you were the caller, and ushered them into our front hall as if you were the doorman. I remember thinking how composed and friendly you were.

"Joel, can you tell us what happened here?" The tall policeman turned slightly sideways and addressed you by name.

"My girlfriend dumped me, and I got so upset I threw our big marble table across the room. It felt like a real emergency, so I called 9-1-1."

"Are you feeling like you might hurt yourself or anyone else, Joel?" His measured tone said the officer had asked this question before.

"Not on purpose. I don't hurt people. I don't like when they tease me, but I don't hurt them. I think I just got so upset about Diana dumping me that I went out of control. She keeps telling me she doesn't want to see me anymore, and I don't get it.... I buy her Tim Hortons Iced Capps and I give her money for her phone cards and I always take her to her bowling and baseball even though I don't like the people she hangs out with there."

"What if you get this upset again?" the cop probed gently.

"Like you mean if Diana dumps me again? I don't think I could stand it.... I really don't know what I'd do."

Now addressing me, the stocky policeman said, "Mrs. Schwartz, those are the magic words. Joel's telling us he's not certain he can control himself, and that means for everyone's good, we're obligated to take him to the hospital."

"Can my mom come with me?" You were beginning to look anxious and started to chew your fingers.

"No, son, but she can come to see you later."

A piece of my broken heart swam up and got stuck in my throat when you asked if Dad and I would visit. Somehow, I managed to deliver your favorite double thumbs up signal. When the tall, dark officer produced a set of handcuffs, I couldn't believe it. You stopped gnawing your hands and stretched your arms out in front of you, but the shorter policeman told you to put your hands behind your back. "Joel, you're a big guy, buddy, and the restraints are for everyone's protection."

You followed his instructions, put your arms behind you while he applied and locked the cuffs. I watched the two officers take you out our front door and lead you down the drive to their patrol car. They guided you into the back seat of the cruiser, shielding your head with their hands. It was the last professional courtesy you ever received.

But for the dog, I was alone. It felt like molasses had filled the void as I struggled to make my way from the front door down the hall to the family room. Piper stopped sniffing for new smells around the foyer and followed me. Once the scene of warmth, comfort, Sesame Street, and WrestleMania, the angled, light-filled room had morphed into a box holding a crushed gift. I managed to sweep up many of the bits and small pieces of marble but couldn't lift the bigger slabs no matter how hard I tried. I gave up and crumpled onto the sofa. Piper stayed at my feet.

Intellectually, I think I had reached a stage where I realized nothing else could be done, but emotionally, I remained driven to keep trying to make things better. It's quite like being on a hamster wheel, and even though you see the bait receding, you run harder and faster trying to reach it. That is what makes it all so sad. Now that I am ten years off that wheel, I see others still on it. I get together with my friends who have adult children with special needs, and I can't advise them to get off because I know in my bones that they can't. They look at me and imagine my grief, and I see them, imagine their struggle, and sometimes reimagine my own. I may well be the lucky one here.

SNOWED

WHEN DAD got home, I had just enough energy to tell him what happened and where you were. He walked into the family room, and while he sifted through the ruins, we agreed there was really nothing more to say or do except call the hospital. I thought I had learned how to "speak doctor" pretty well from listening to Pop-Pop tell us about his hospital rounds and from some summer jobs I had there. I gathered my confidence and dialed the main number.

"My name is Julie Schwartz, and my son Joel was taken to Sunnybrook by the police, and I would like to check on his status."

"Just a moment."

Many moments later: "We don't have him in hospital."

"Did you check the Emergency Room?"

"Just a moment."

Many moments later: "They don't have him in a room."

"Could you please put me through to the ER?"

"Just a moment."

"Sunnybrook ER."

"I'm calling to check on Joel Schwartz who was brought to the ER by the police late this afternoon."

"Are you a relative?"

"I am his mother."

"Just a moment.... Mrs. Schwartz, we don't have a room for Joel, and he has not been assessed yet."

"Where is he, and may I speak with him?"

"He is with the police in the hallway, and we don't recommend speaking with him now."

"Will the police stay with him until he is seen by the doctor?"

"Depending on how long it takes."

"Would it be possible for us to speak with the doctor once Joel is assessed?"

"We can try to arrange that."

"Will the senior psychiatry resident assess him?"

"The doctor on duty in the ER will see him."

I insisted they note your psychiatrist's name and your allergy to Risperidone.

"I will make a note of that information on his chart."

"And can you please let us know once he has been assessed?"

"It's best if you call back to check."

"Should we come to the hospital?"

"Better to wait for now."

Dad decided to lie down. I spent the next two hours trying to find some breath. I paced the house rearranging photos and straightening closets and wondering how it could be that we were at home and you had been taken away by the POLICE? The police are the ones we ask for directions when we're lost, the ones we call on for help, the ones who track down the bad guys, the ones who interact with people on the wrong side of the law. How was it that we came to have police in our house when we hadn't done anything wrong or even been robbed? Maybe we had been broken into.

ও

It was getting late and I called again. When I finally reached the doctor, the first thing he told me was that you were not psychotic and that they had given you Risperidone to "calm you down." I think my response may have shattered his eardrum. You had been given that drug once before and all its negative side effects kicked in and made you twitch and grimace uncontrollably. It may have calmed you down, but it made you look the opposite of calm. When he heard that, the doctor promised to reverse the order for Risperidone immediately.

Back and forth. Back and forth. We were finally told that you would be admitted to Sunnybrook once a bed became available in the Psychiatry Unit, but that might not be till the morning. We were advised to call back then. It felt like you were an astronaut who had entered that period of radio silence when the space capsule leaves Earth's atmosphere.

You were admitted to F-Wing on Dr. X's service, even though you were an outpatient of Dr. Q. The care model didn't seem to connect inpatient and outpatient physicians at the same hospital, for the same person. Dad and I were told to wait a few days before visiting so that you could get used to the routine. With Jonathan in Montreal and you in the hospital, we bumped into each other pacing around the house. It was very quiet, and the air seemed still and dead without you. Maybe it was just a masquerade, but I had an odd sense of relief thinking you were under control in a safe place. Piper didn't know what to do with himself and roamed from room to room sniffing for you.

We called F-Wing several times a day, were told you were comfortable and doing well, but had no concept of what that meant. Waiting to be able to see you felt like being strong-armed at bay by an invisible opponent. I avoided as many people as I could. I couldn't stand them asking how things were going, and I busied myself imagining outrageous responses: *Oh, Joel is doing fine. His straitjacket fits well, and they let him choose the color he wanted.*

Three days after our family room imploded, we were finally permitted to visit you. At the hospital we found our way through the labyrinth to the psychiatric unit, which was located as far as possible from the main entrance. The world may have come a long way, but the health care geography implies it's still the loony bin. When we checked in at the nurses' station, we were directed down the hall to your room. There, we saw four single beds, one of which had a larva-like lump curled up and glued atop a thin blue-ticked mattress. It was unwashed, unshaven, and its legs were covered with your favorite, dirty John Deere flannel pajama bottoms. I realized then that you hadn't changed into street clothes when the police took you away.

Dad asked what bed you were in, and I pointed to you.

I went over and whispered into your crusted ear. "JoJo, it's Mom." Dad patted your shoulder and told you we were there to visit.

Then he said it again louder.

Nothing.

The nurse advised us not to expect too much because you were heavily sedated. I had once heard that the medical lingo for "heavily sedated" was "snowed"— just like the street slang for an overdose of heroin.

Whether or not you could hear him, Dad tried hard to reassure you and himself that all would be well again once you came home.

We came each of the next few days to see you but witnessed no change and no doctor. A kind nurse explained that her own daughter had gone through a bad break-up and that "these things take time." When we inquired about getting you showered and shaved, a different attendant cheerfully chirped that you could have a shower, and that we could bring you some clothes, but no shave because "we don't allow sharpies on this unit."

And then, as if an unseen magician waved a wand, on our next visit we found you up and eating dinner with other patients in a small light-filled room. You were beaming and got up to greet us, and that's when we saw that Diana was at the table. She stayed seated, smiled, and said hello as if nothing had happened, then helped herself to your dinner—it looked like peas, potatoes, and some meat. We could easily all have been in a family restaurant. There was pleasant chatter among the patients and visitors, and everyone but us looked at ease. They all seemed to know Diana, and we found out that she had been coming to see you every day. Dad and I were astonished, but so relieved to see you up and eating that we didn't say a word. The friendly nurse said you had made a remarkable recovery and would be released soon, and that the hospital would schedule a discharge conference.

Your transformation from sedated, filthy, and unresponsive to alert, clean, and pleasant was mind-boggling. Dad and I were still standing but reeling. We had been through all the ups and downs of your life, but never anything like this. The only other time you were in hospital was for a minor day surgery to correct your lazy left eye when you were two. If mothers are hard-wired to nurture and dads are meant to protect, then how did you end up here, and how did you get better without us? The whole equation seemed unbalanced, and everything was out of kilter. No longer catalysts and advocates, we had turned into bystanders. Years of patience, support, care, and devotion simply seemed trumped by the mystery of love. It was nerve-racking, and very difficult to be confident in your recovery, knowing Diana was still in the picture.

F-WING DISCHARGE

EVERY WEDNESDAY I attend the Mindfulness-Based Cognitive Therapy Program held in the F-Wing of Sunnybrook Hospital. Small world. The door to F-Wing is just beyond the Emergency Room entrance. Each time I go by, I check for ambulances being unloaded and silently wish them good luck. When the F-Wing outer door is locked, I have to enter the hospital through the Emergency Room Walk-In entrance. I hold my breath while I walk through, and I walk through quickly. It seems to me a cruel test of strength, but one I have conquered. Once in F-Wing, I head down the office-lined corridors to the room where Mindfulness meets. One night early on in the program, I came face-to-face with the psychiatrist who had treated Joel on an outpatient basis and was in the ER the evening he died. When I said hello, his eyes got big and his face went white. "What are you doing here?" he stammered.

"I'm in the therapeutic Mindfulness Program," I answered. He recovered enough to ask me if I found it helpful. "Oh, yes," I said. "You should try it."

Dad and I were ushered into the F-Wing Family Conference Room to find you shaved, showered, and in street clothes for the first time in seven days. There was an awkward group hug, and then we stood waiting for the doctors while you chewed your fingers and asked to call Diana. The room was an oversized cubicle posing as a living room, but the pale-green walls and industrial furniture gave it away—along with an unpleasant mix of medicinal smells and stale air.

While in hospital, you were on Dr. X's service, and he swept into the conference room with his pale Russian assistant in tow. He announced in his crisp South African accent that he only had twenty minutes. His formality and urgency left me feeling your case was unworthy of his time. My right eyelid began to twitch.

We were instructed to join you and sit across the

table. He called on the resident to present a summary of your treatment. With her husky accent she pushed each word out as if it were a heavy rock. I leaned in, trying to focus, but I imagined how hard it must have been for you to understand her.

Did you? It felt more like a year-end business report than a treatment summary of a vulnerable human being. Dad sat with his arms crossed and eyes glazed. You fidgeted, and inside I was seething with anger.

The meeting came to an abrupt end, and ignoring us, the psychiatrist turned to you and announced, "Joel, I'd like you to know that you've had a very real problem managing your anger, and you are quite impulsive, but there is no evidence that you have a mental illness."

After an entire week in a drugged state of one-syllable grunts, you brightened for a moment and said, "Well, I guess the good news is I'm not crazy."

My shoulders automatically relaxed at the sound of your voice, and I swallowed a laugh. The psychiatrist didn't miss a beat and barked out detailed discharge plans, calling for occupational therapy, anger management therapy, talk therapy, and pharmaceutical interventions; and he said the hospital would be in touch to arrange all this.

The doctors owned the entire meeting, granting

no time for questions from any of us. Dr. X quickly concluded the session and, without a second thought, offered a summary pronouncement directed at you: "Joel, we have doubled the dose of one of your medicines and are adding a new medicine for you because taking more medicine will make you feel better."

Rising from his chair, he excused himself and left for his next conference. The resident stayed and tried to explain that the hospital pharmacy could fill the prescriptions. As we gathered you and ourselves together and moved into the hall, Dad and I finally realized that she had wished us "good luck."

On the way to the pharmacy, you stopped for a minute and said, "Mom, if the doctor said I'm not crazy, why was I in F-Wing? Everyone knows F-Wing is for people who are fucked up."

VITAL SIGNS ABSENT

I REMEMBER IT was a Tuesday when you called to say you had the afternoon off since you got all your deliveries done in the morning. It was around two in the afternoon, and you said you were going home to take a nap. When I arrived, the house was quiet, and your shoes were at the door. I went grocery shopping and when I came back, my friend dropped off photos of our trip to Israel. After she left, I noticed a blue-and-white EMS van idling in front of the Zucker's house. I remember feeling bad that poor Mr. Zucker probably had another heart attack. I went to our side door to bring in the mail and found it open and surrounded with piles of stained, rumpled, orange blankets. I bolted to the EMS van, and it was running but empty. Through the driver's window I saw that the computer screen read: MALE-25 yrs.

My phone rang again, and this time it was Dad screaming at me to come to Sunnybrook because you had had a seizure. I cannot recall how I got to the hospital, but a lady in a pink smock, the color of Pepto-Bismol, stopped me as I rushed into the Emergency Room. I told her your name and that I had to see you. Though very kind and calm, she would not let me through the doors to the treatment area. Instead, she led me down the hall—away from the place where they save lives, to the quiet room where they tell you they did everything they could and are very sorry for your loss.

I began to feel like I was watching us all on TV. The mother in the show seemed calm and stoic. My heart went out to the father as he sobbed and shook. The young man on the stretcher looked very peaceful, but had food bits crusted around his lips and a tube still stuck in his mouth. The nurse apologized about the mess and warned the mom that the floor was still slippery from when they pumped the young man's stomach. The mother held her son's hand. Was he ever going to stop biting his nails? She saw that one of his eyes was a little open, closed it, and sat with him until the nurses said it was time for her to leave.

The TV show ended abruptly when the coroner showed the mother the empty bottles of medicine the EMS guys found at the house and said that her son had consumed a fatal dose.

I numbly walked back toward the sad, wood-paneled dark room where Dad was sobbing and the EMT team and ER doctor had gathered to mumble condolences. I wanted them to know that we believed they had all done their best and made a point of telling them so. It seemed only fair to let them off the hook.

At the hospital, death is death for only a moment. Then the post-death workings begin. Will organs or body parts be donated? Will there be an autopsy? Where will the body be moved to? Who will call the funeral home and notify the rabbi? When and how will family and friends be told?

Somehow all this happened, and we exited the hospital right next to where you had entered it. The evening was very still. Dad had followed the ambulance in our car so we walked to the parking lot and found where he had ditched it. Slapped under the windshield wiper was a yellow parking ticket. Clearly, we had overstayed our welcome. While Dad started the car, I removed the ticket, ripped it up, and watched the pieces flutter to the ground. Then we drove home. Piper seemed especially relieved to see us when we came in the front door.

Jonathan had arrived home from university at midnight, and none of us slept. Something absolutely impossible had happened. It was not logical, and it could not be true. Yet, strangely enough, the next morning we found ourselves going to the funeral home. The director ushered us into a room, invited us to sit down, and brought a Bassett Hound into the room hoping that "petting it would give us some comfort." He was professional and gently asked which of our parents had passed. He fell apart when we said it was our son. The dog went over and sat at his feet. When he pulled himself together, he took us to the casket room so that we could select a coffin to hold your body for eternity. On the way, he explained the different casing options, some water repellant and others not, and then ushered us into a vault with about fifty different styles laid out for us to inspect. He left us alone for a while. A man in a dark suit stood guard by the door. He looked like Uncle Fester from the *Addams Family*.

There were so many options that it was like shopping for furniture; and when Dad looked at one very flimsy-looking casket, Jonathan told him we were not going to send you underground in an IKEA box. There was another one made of mahogany with lots of ornate carvings. We giggled out loud thinking that someone rich and famous would be heading underground in that one. In the end, we chose one for you that is the same as Zaidy's—plain, dignified, and made of pine with a Star of David carved on top.

The funeral director returned. Perhaps the man at the door had signaled to him that we had made our choice. He informed us the Jewish star could be removed if we liked. We asked that it be left in place. Your recent and only visit to Israel had given you a remarkable boost, so why not remind God you were among his chosen.

When I got to see you again, the prayer shawl you wore at your Bar Mitzvah was draped around your face. The coffin was open because someone needed to confirm that it was you. Jonathan looked, called out your name, and made a noise somewhere between a scream and a sob. Dad didn't look. A man from the funeral home asked me if I wanted to stay while he performed the last rituals. I did. He made a little pillow full of sand from Israel and put it under your head. He placed a pebble on each of your eyes and told me they would prevent you from being blinded by the light when the Messiah came to lead you and the others back. Since you never went anywhere without your TTC Metropass, I left you your new one from March 2009, along with a stone from Massada to remind you of how much fun you had in Israel, and a piece of paper with Mel's cell phone number. He says you can call him whenever you like.

Almost a thousand people came to say good-bye to you. The funeral at Holy Blossom Temple was like a reception for a guest of honor who couldn't attend. Jonathan told everyone how humbled and lucky he was to be your brother, even though he knows you thought he was a pain in the ass. He read "Forever Young." He said living with you taught him everything he will ever need to know, and that with you not here, it feels like half our family is gone. The cantor sang beautifully, and the rabbi talked about your goodness, honesty, loyalty, and wonderful sense of humor. He made people smile when he said that if you wanted to be someone's friend, they had no choice in the matter. Dad and I asked everyone to think of you often and to be kind to people who are different.

We had our heads in the clouds preparing an obituary for you and our feet on the ground buying a plot to put you in. Realizing it would be more sensible, we bought three: one for you, Dad, and me. Then we had to decide on the order in which our bodies would be buried. My first idea was to put you in the middle and then Dad and me on either side, like when you were little and would climb into our bed to snuggle between us. But then we figured to put you at one end with whoever died next beside you, and the one after that next in order. Probably best to have me and Dad next to each other anyway. Jonathan wanted to know why we didn't buy a place for him. We explained that by the time it's his turn to die, he will have a spot with the family he makes, rather than with the one that made him.

There is a Jewish custom that all who wish to may shovel earth onto the coffin once it has been lowered into the ground. This is considered the purist form of a good deed because the dead person can never pay the shoveler back, and thus, the act is deemed completely selfless. Who knows? But it sounds good. After everyone had a turn, Jonathan continued shoveling and would not leave till there was a mound of earth that rose well above the perimeter of the grave itself.

When I was walking back to the limousine, a religiously observant man approached me to offer his condolences. He told me he had lost a five-year-old grandson several years ago and hoped it would comfort me to know that God sends very special people into the world and leaves them here just long enough for them to have a positive impact on the rest of us before he calls them back to heaven. He said he thought that you, like his grandson, might be one of those angels.

THE BEST MAN

WHEN I THINK of us as a family of four, I wonder about luck and what it is and what it isn't. What is good luck made of, and what causes luck to go bad? Was your being born with a developmental disability a stroke of misfortune or luck? I torment myself by imagining that maybe someone or something is in charge of meting out luck and that there is a court of appeal. Then I picture myself in lawyer robes, pleading our case and presenting a closing argument. If luck took a holiday when you were born, she certainly came back and paid us plenty of visits.

Jonathan was the perfect brother for you. It was almost like he was prescribed for our family. Four years your junior, he was an undeniable presence who wormed his way into your heart despite all you did to let him know you did not want a brother. Weighing a full ten pounds at birth, Jonathan delighted the maternity nurses who all said he looked like a three-month-old baby. In addition to his girth, he came equipped with all the extra social antennae you had been denied. It was as if some power that looked away when you were born came back and glanced at him, and paid back the difference owed. Your brother was a patient, kind, and firm instructor who instinctively knew to show rather than to tell you what to do.

Soon after he was born, Dad and I began to notice the ease with which your brother breezed through the developmental markers you had struggled to meet. He was smiling, gurgling, and crawling in no time; and he was a charmer from the get-go. "Ahhh," I said to Dad, "this must be what they mean when they say 'normal.'" Jonathan had my mother, who was usually in charge of everything, wrapped around his tiny finger, and when she asked him to make "goo-goo" eyes, he batted his lashes at her and giggled. He was a puppy, determined to follow you everywhere.

Whenever he lost your trail he would holler: "JoJo, I WANT you!"

Just outside his vision, you once asked me: "Why does he want ME when he has so many toys?"

"He just wants to play with you."

"Well I would rather play with my trains, and he isn't allowed to touch them. Besides, he doesn't do what I tell him like my trains do."

But your brother's sixth sense about you kicked in, and he would bring his tiny toy-train cars into your room and sit at the other end of the bed and play. Little by little, he would inch his trains over near you and then ask you to tell him about each one. You would read him the specs, and he would listen and ask more and more questions so you would let him stay with you.

Dad and I worked very hard to model appropriate conversations and show you how to pay attention by "looking into the other person's eyes" when you talk with them. Since you rarely made eye contact, a speech pathologist suggested we cup your chin and gently turn your face toward whoever was speaking to you. I was blown away one night at dinner when Jonathan was trying to talk to you, and you were facing in the opposite direction. He got out of his booster seat, went behind your chair, cupped your chin, and staring you down said, "JoJo, you have to yook in mine eyes when we talking."

Over time, it was painful to see that Jonathan was surpassing you in many areas. How can the older brother be behind the younger one? Well, Jonathan had a solution for that as well. He managed to focus on all the things you could do better than he could for as long as possible; and he sought your help whenever possible. Even in high school he would defer to your superior spelling and geography and map skills, finding you a ready-made answer-man when Dad would try to get him to use the dictionary instead. You found spelling so easy and natural, you said you could never figure out why Jonathan had trouble with it.

Dad and I loved eavesdropping whenever we could overhear you guys talking together. "Jonathan how come you have so many more friends than I do?"

"Because I call them and ask them to get together to do things I know they like to do."

"But I don't like to do the things other people do."

"Maybe you'd like to do more things if you would try more things."

"Is there anything else I can do to have as many friends as you?"

"Yup."

"What else?"

"Stop picking your nose."

Once, Jonathan crept into our bedroom and started to sob. Adolescence has something special in store for each of us, and for as much as he was your shepherd, he was still your little brother.

Dad and I sat on our bed with him until he was able to speak. In between sobs he wanted to know: "How will I ever be able to make enough money to take care of Joel for the rest of our lives when you are gone?" Somehow, it seemed to us to mean that he knew we were all in this together with you.

Our attempts to relieve his anxiety were pretty clumsy, but what we told him was that putting together enough money to look after you was our job and not his. We went on to say that our hope was that he would continue to be a good brother to you and that he would live a good life including you as much as possible. This is something he still does.

Knowing you weren't supposed to go into his room never stopped you. Once, after your evening snoop, Dad and Jonathan and I were at the table when you came down late for dinner and asked, "Mom, how come Jonathan has a driver's license with another boy's picture and a different birthday?"

"Joel, what were you doing in my room?"

"Nothing."

"Then how do you know about that?"

"I just saw it on your desk. How come you have it?"

"Never mind."

Dad woke up and asked, "Jonathan, exactly what

kind of license do you have and what do you plan to do with it?"

"Nothing, and Joel shouldn't have gone into my room."

"Well do you have a fake license up there? Yes or no?"

"It's just for one night."

"What do you mean?"

"Yoni and I are meeting Ryan and Michael to go watch the Leafs semi-final game."

"So why do you need a fake license to watch TV?"

"Dad, we're going to watch it at Shoeless Joe's."

"Isn't that a sports bar?"

"That's why I need the license…to use for ID…. We're not going to drink, just watch the game on the big screen."

"And how did you get the other boy's license?"

"It's called a scratch, and you can buy them."

"Is that what you did?"

"Yes."

"Bring it down here now."

"Dad, it's just for one night."

"Bring it here and get me the scissors."

"Oh, Jonathan, I think I got you in big trouble."

"You sure did."

"Will you ever forgive me?"

"Eventually, but just leave me alone now."

"I'll get your phony license for Dad right now," you volunteered, hoping to be of help.

§

Who knows what luck really means? I do believe it's lucky that you no longer suffer the challenges brought on by difference, and that you died knowing you are loved, and that Dad was with you as you left. I think we are lucky that Jonathan rooted for you, Joel. He loved you and wanted everything to go well for you. Even though you never made it to his and Jordanna's wedding, everyone knows you will always be Jonathan's best man.

He hated Diana for you because he saw her as your downfall. He sent you funny postcards from camp; and he often wrote you letters and notes of encouragement. Do you remember the one he gave you when he was home for semester break, and you were nervous to leave for Israel right before your Birthright trip?

Dear Joel,

Great to see you, as always. Sorry it was a short-lived visit. I just want you to know how much I love you and how much the entire family loves you. YOU choose your own fate with Israel. It is a beautiful place and not something to pass up on, especially when it's free! We will all be here for you when you get back! Think of how proud Zaidy and Pop-Pop would be if they saw you take such a big step in your life at twenty-five years of age. Impress yourself and go, and if people are friendly and you make some friends, all the better—if not, screw them and enjoy Israel in all its glory. Either way, we all love you and you have grown so much already, this would just be another big step, of which you have taken many!

Love always,
Jonathan

You came home from the Birthright experience bursting with pride and a new group of peers who appreciated you just for being you. We had arranged for a "shadow" for you, and Emmanuel was terrific. He was your "roommate" and subltly guided you through the social landscape and encouraged you to express your wonderful sense of humor. Dave, the group leader, made it his mission to have you included and enjoyed by others on the trip; and extending that inclusion to fill up your social calendar with invitations to parties and other gatherings from the time you got home until Diana broke up with you. After you died, the Birthright gang put together a book of rememberances and photos from the trip and gave it to our family. Dave and I still go for walks together and talk about you.

CORRECT TENSE

ARE YOU or were you, Joel? Your name is etched in a granite stone above a grave. Is that where you are now? You are gone. Though gone doesn't automatically mean dead, dead does mean gone. Although—maybe not. Perhaps you are merely not present, or maybe you are present in another form or another way. You may not be alive in the sense you once were, but you can be alive as a memory as long as someone who knew you is still living. So, you might not be dead and gone until the youngest person to have ever met you dies. When there is no one left to recall, what difference will it make anyway?

Do you have ASD, or *did* you have it? Did it follow you into the ground or disappear when you died? We threw out all the diagnostic reports that pigeon-holed you into a DSM (Diagnostic and Statistical Manual) cubby, funneled you into special education classes, and shadowed you wherever you went. We all tried valiantly to focus on your abilities, and no one tried harder than you. So, what happens to ASD when you and the test results are gone?

You were such a pain in the ass with all your repeated questions, but we're the ones with questions now. And you were so clumsy, but not anymore. The house is very still now, nothing is in danger of being broken, and everything is in its place. But you are missing, and we are missing you. You were always so affectionate— now your hugs seem to come from the inside out. Are you still funny or did you stop being funny when you stopped being? You do still make us laugh. Here's a joke you might like: Are you having the time of your life, or are you having the time of your death?

May I say you *are* kind and generous, or do I have to say you *were* determined, good humored, and honest to a fault?

Do you or did you have curly hair? If curly is relative to straight, what does death do to curly? Do you need a haircut? Has it grown to a full 'fro, or has it gone completely? Can everything you did have actually ended with you? We still have all the proof: licenses, diplomas, unpaid traffic tickets, VHF operator card, Air Cadet wings. Crazy that the only paper that counts is the one that says you are dead. How could a person be a brother, son, Bar Mitzvah, and then not be one? Are you Jewish, or were you? Does death steal identity and erase belief?

You lived and died loving trains, planes, stars, buses, and dogs. Did you love Piper or do you? He looked for you for days after you died. When he stopped looking for you, he started looking like you—wolfing down food then belching, pawing us for attention, and thundering up and down the stairs. I caught myself smiling one winter day when he scarfed some new snow just like you used to. Piper turned eleven this year, and I am worried that when he dies, it might feel like losing you all over again. I may smack anyone who tries to cheer me up by suggesting that I can "always get another one."

When I go down to the basement to do laundry in the room next to yours, I wonder if any of your breaths are still in our house? If matter can't be created or destroyed, where did your last breath go? I found one of your wisdom teeth in an old 35 mm film cartridge and thought about how the dentist and I bribed you to let him knock you out by letting you hold the keys to his Mercedes. It was weird holding your tooth, and it does feel strange to have an actual part of your body, full of your DNA, in the drawer of a desk where you did homework, but I guess lots of parents save their children's teeth. I know a woman who is so desperate to feel close to her daughter that she gilded the girl's tooth and made it into an earring that she wears and touches so she can feel near to her. The daughter is alive and well and living nearby.

Here's a crazy idea I had: Maybe when I die, they could cut out my heart and find room for it in your coffin. I hope Daddy isn't insulted to know I want my heart to be with you. Maybe he would understand. I don't know how much of you will be left in your pine box by the time I die, but I imagine whatever of you is there no longer fills it up the way you did when all of you went into it. Some of you must have disintegrated by now—maybe enough so that there will be room for a heart that is smaller than it used to be.

When you were born, I became your mother. An awful lot has changed, but I am and will always be that.

ROOTS AND WINGS

NOT THAT LONG before Joel died, we renovated our kitchen in order to bring it into modern times.

My favorite part of the tricky process of remodeling was getting to choose the granite that would become our counter tops. Because it came near the end of the exercise, it seemed like a reward for all the thankless decisions about appliances and pantry measurements. I loved going to the warehouse and walking up and down the aisles that housed huge flat hunks of stone that had been dug from the earth like giant fossils. The veining and marbling on each piece seemed to tell a story, and I was fascinated by the variety of colors and patterns. Finally, I settled on a slab that seemed simultaneously neutral and exciting. It was a mixture of warm taupes and vanillas interspersed with bits of brown that made it look like it was choked with mini Hershey's Kisses. It fit perfectly into our new décor, and it is impossible to destroy.

A few years after choosing our kitchen counter granite, Larry and I were tasked once again with selecting a slab of granite, this time for Joel's headstone. I think the irony may have made us giddy, and we ruled out the salmon-colored option as being too feminine and even managed to chuckle telling each other that Joel would have probably called us out, yelling "PINK, why did you choose PINK.... PINK is for girls!"

We agreed that shiny black was out of the question because there was nothing about Joel that was shiny or black...two adjectives that are way too elegant for him or anything about his life. Then the choice was down to light gray stone, shiny or matte finish, with lettering etched in black; or charcoal gray stone, shiny or matte finish, with lettering etched in light gray. We continued to agree completely that the darker gray matte finished stone with light lettering was the best choice since it seemed to make a strong impression without calling attention to itself or showing off. As well, we felt the light gray stone seemed to be for an older, paler person.

Larry and I divided the job of what to say on the headstone in accordance with what we each did best.

He took care of creating the Hebrew inscription, and I wrote the English wording. The Hebrew had to conform to certain traditional parameters, and I wanted the English to capture the essence of Joel. I took great care in coming up with an inscription that would be a little different from the usual, but still serious and respectful. I wanted the words to be about Joel and not about the fact that I wrote them…and since there is no editing once the copy is approved, I really wanted to get it right. I envisioned anyone visiting the cemetery, years into the future, stopping at Joel's grave and saying to themselves, *This is someone I would like to have known.*

So, in addition to the Hebrew, which states among other things Joel's Hebrew name, birth and death dates, and that he is the son of Larry and Julie, the English wording says: "Beloved son, brother, grandson, nephew, friend, and very human being." I still think of these words as the best ones I have ever written.

Larry and I once attended a parenting group where the leader explained that parenting was hard because the challenge was essentially a paradox, since "children need both roots and wings." I imagined a tree with wings instead of branches and thought about trying to simultaneously put down roots and sprout limbs to fly. It certainly seemed impossible to me until

I took *simultaneously* out of the equation and reminded myself that there were two of us to meet this challenge.

As a careful, analytical person, Larry usually watched and waited before weighing in on any problem or issue. In Larry, Joel and Jonathan had a well-rooted father who taught by example and whose behavior demonstrated what was right. He consistently showed what was right by doing what was right. As a dyed-in-the-wool fixer, I was a mother whose default was to jump right in and try to find solutions. I wished Larry would see and notice more and wait less. I think Larry hoped I would do less and wait to see what might happen more. For better or worse, though, while I was flying around pursuing the magic bullet that would make Joel better and taking Jonathan for extra skating so he could make select hockey, Larry stayed put and was the wall that didn't move. He was a reliable, steadfast presence that Joel and Jonathan could bump into again and again in all their conscious and unconscious efforts to test limits. The wall didn't move or bend or cater to disability but stood firm, fueled with love and patience.

Parenting is such a big job that even if you have a playbook, there just isn't time to read it during the game. Reading it ahead of time might give you a head start, but ultimately, you do a lot of flying by the seat of your pants. As it turns out, I think Larry and I are very lucky that our two different approaches to the same desired outcome may have accidently helped Joel and Jonathan develop roots and wings.

In the months after Joel died, Larry read and prayed and slept and worked. I walked and did and did and walked. We were together and apart at the same time, two stunned and shocked people being polite and awkwardly caring. We enacted the "activities of daily life" like robots. We never avoided each other or "the topic," nor did we seek each other out to discuss Joel's death; although I did once ask Larry if he had any sense of guilt about not being able to save Joel when he found him in the basement. He told me that, on the contrary, he felt fortunate to know that Joel knew he was there and never left him. This answer was a huge relief for me. Whenever Joel or his absence came up in conversation, we acknowledged it and reassured each other we would be okay because, really, was there any other option? After all, there was life to live even though death had visited.

A year after Joel was buried, it was time to place and unveil his headstone. Larry's words at the ceremony were stunning and remarkable given that we were gathered at the grave of our son. I was in awe as he talked about it being time to move from the agony of grief to the poignancy of memory—to begin to ease away from mourning Joel's death and focus on remembering his life.

Well into our relationship, and even through several years of marriage, I thought of Larry and I as being the same height even though I knew he was taller. He once made me stand next to him in front of a mirror to prove reality. Larry always carried himself comfortably, and at six foot two he definitely qualifies as tall. On the day of Joel's unveiling I thought of Larry as a tower. I can't think of anyone I know who I respect or admire more.

THE RUG

I WOULD LIKE to requisition a change of status but be permitted to retain what I have learned from my situation. I no longer want to be the mother of a dead child. It's enough already. I have done a good job toeing the bereaved mother line. I have avoided taking advantage of what it can afford. I have not wallowed; I am simply fed up and would like a new assignment. Most of what I know I learned by living. It can be shared but not taught because it only sinks in via experience. Facts and general information can be taught and learned. Wisdom, on the other hand, comes from experience. I used to wonder whether it would be better to be smart or wise. I've concluded that smart simply hurts less.

I wanted to avoid Joel's disability having a negative impact on other people; and it made me very uncomfortable to think that another child's experience would be in any way compromised because of Joel's needs. While I always wanted him to be included, I never wanted that to happen at anyone else's expense. He and his needs were, first and foremost, our responsibility. Interestingly enough, the same is true of his death. It is a big fact that belongs to us and when others find out or think about it, it can stop them in their tracks. Just like his life, his death is a huge responsibility that has to be managed.

Certain times of the year are harder than others, but it seems to have little to do with the season. Happy can come more easily on a sunny winter day than on a summer one overhung with heavy clouds. But it isn't the weather either. A smile can be coaxed by a single raindrop clinging to a twig or a perfect pattern of snow driven onto a chain-link fence.

Sad can stage an ambush at a birthday party, seep into a light and pleasing conversation, or permeate a picnic. It can plummet heavily down the mineshaft and settle deep, or just as easily float away and dissolve in a gentle breeze.

᪣

I was relieved that Jonathan went back to Montreal to finish his last year at McGill once the shiva for you ended. When he asked the rabbi what he was supposed to do now that you were gone, the answer came from the essence of Judaism—"Choose life." In other words, the rabbi told Jonathan that as the more fortunate of two brothers, his job was to now live the most positive life possible in your honor, rather than torment himself in your memory. With you gone and Jonathan away, the house was empty but for Dad, me, and the dog. Friends dropped by to keep me busy, and Dad read, slept, and went to shul. The dog spent days racing up and down the basement stairs looking for you. We knew what happened, but even with the power of reason, we didn't understand it.

Poor Piper didn't even know what happened let alone understand it. Instead, he sniffed the perimeter of your room in the basement over and over searching for traces of you. When I noticed he was out of sight for longer than normal, I'd go down to find him curled at the foot of your bed—nose to tail the way dogs do when they tuck themselves in for the night.

Remember how wild he was when I first brought him home? He galloped up to you and practically bowled you over. I had been told he was house-trained, but later that day you hollered to me to "come see the pile of shit the dog dumped in my room." Little by little Piper calmed down, and when he finally learned to sit nicely, he'd do that at your side and put his paw up on your leg, and you'd tell me you could feel his claws massaging your knee as if he were begging for even more attention. He was a big and woolly nine-month-old standard poodle I adopted from a lady who didn't want him anymore because he was tan and black. He was way different from our first dog…the big white poodle we got as a puppy when you were around six. That was when Dad was supposed to go on a business trip to Uganda for five weeks, and I thought we could pick up the puppy and have him trained and settled in by the time Dad got back. It might have worked, but when Dad's trip got postponed, my scheme backfired. Dad was a good sport though, and we kept the puppy.

You named the white poodle Hunter because you had looked up poodles and found out that the big ones were originally used for hunting and retrieving birds. We always said that the dog had the classiest name in our family, but it was a bit of an oxymoron: Hunter Schwartz.

As affectionate and affable as Piper is, was how aloof Hunter was. You and Jonathan would pet him, and he would tolerate it for a bit and then get up and politely walk away. Jonathan would leave him alone, but somehow you couldn't. He never growled or snarled, but he made it clear he was not interested in your affection; and you continued to pursue him. Finally, it dawned on me that I could use the dog as a concrete example to teach you about the two-way nature of relationships, looking for signs and signals of how the other person (in this case the dog) is feeling, and the idea of letting others come to you. When Hunter eventually died, you and Jonathan took it very hard. Dad didn't want another dog, and I knew I had to have one, but waited for five years before I got Piper. He never could get enough of you and always pushed his head or backed his bum into you to ask for pats and hugs. You absolutely loved when he did that, and so did I. You could wrap him in a bear hug, and he'd sit for as long as you wanted to hold him.

Piper still fits into the rhythm of my days even though you don't. It's not that I don't think of you, because I always do. It's just that you don't need me anymore. Meanwhile, I feed, brush, and walk the dog and find these tasks calming and his company reassuring. Jonathan roughhouses with him, and even Dad takes him for walks. They would go to visit Bubbie at Pine Villa, and all the old people would ask to pet the dog and talked to him in their original languages. Bubbie had a hard time telling Dad and Uncle Ricky apart anymore, but she always recognized Piper and called him by name. Once, she asked me if Piper was married. When I told her dogs don't get married, she wondered out loud, "Then how do they have puppies?"

You were working as a courier when you decided you were ready to move out and live on your own. We found a decent, affordable one-bedroom apartment in a solid brick building from the 1930s. It was a walkable distance from our house, which meant we were out of sight, but available as a perpetual safety net. We went to IKEA to get furniture, and you eagerly planned where you would put your desk, computer, and bus, train, and airplane model collections. I was in charge of the boring but necessary items like cleaning products and accessories. The landlord gave the place a new coat of fresh white paint that covered most of the wall blemishes and made the place look clean and new-ish. But the bathroom gave away the apartment's age. The sink, toilet, tub, and tiles were a combination of chalky pink and purple, and the walls were painted to match. These colors hailed from that era that broke away from black and white in an ill-advised effort at glamor; and you were focused on why they gave you a "pink bathroom." Despite everything, I found a rug for that room that was such a perfect match that it elevated it to high kitsch. The thing had a brown edge framing an arrangement of every purple vegetable and fruit known to man; eggplants, plums, grapes, and figs danced together encircled by a leafy vine. It cost twenty-two dollars, and that sealed the deal.

About three weeks before moving day, you changed your mind, saying you were too nervous to be totally on your own yet. We tried to convince you that you could do it, but your panic levels were rising, and the antici-pation was too hard to bear. We decided you could live in the basement as an interim step toward independence. Fortunately, the landlord was able to rent the place again and most of what we had purchased for the apartment could be used at home—except the bath-room rug, which was completely alien to any décor in our house. I went from room to room trying to find a place for it. Doing that put me in mind of all the times I visited schools and programs and camps looking for places where you might fit in. I could not bring myself to throw the rug away in hopes that keeping it might mean that one day you would need it to match an-other pink and purple bathroom in another apartment in a 1930s solid brick building. So I wrapped it up and stored it in the basement. After you died, I finally did find a spot for it on the landing at the top of the base-ment stairs.

That's where it is now. The nap is crushed down from years of traffic and the colors are faded, but still true to the original hues that were so right for that bathroom and so wrong for our house. I step on it every morning when I get the dog his food from the cupboard on the landing. I like when the rug's edge is flush with the threshold of the basement door, keeping it company the whole way across. When it's uneven, I jockey the rug into place tight against the doorjamb so that no light or floor color seeps between. Piper watches expectantly. I feed him, watch him scarf down his kibble, and think of you.

EPILOGUE
Julie Since Joel

I read that if you change the way you look at life, you change the life you look at. I wonder if I can change Joel's death by changing the way I look at it. So, what would changing my view of Joel's death look like? If I continue to view it as a tragedy, that's where it remains. If I see it statically as the end of opportunities and possibilities, then it stands as just that and nothing more. But if I can consider Joel's life for what it was, and focus on all it yielded, then I can see it as a decent life that ended too soon but left lasting positive results. Then it is possible for me to look at Joel's death as a punctuation mark in the phenomenon that was, and still is, him. So, his death becomes a pause rather than an ending.

Joel David Schwartz was honesty, determination, decency, and good humor writ large. He had ASD, and his life was filled with the peaks and valleys brought on by the unusual talents and challenges that accompany this developmental disability. He was literal and concrete in his thinking and awkward and clumsy in his attempts to socialize. My life became devoted to catching him up and desperately trying to "normalize" him; and I was like a dog with a bone about doing that. Until it finally came to me that it would be much better for everyone if I learned how to help him be the best of who he was, rather than attempting to turn him into someone he just wasn't.

Children eventually leave home, but when death takes them away, it contravenes the natural order. It stuns, outrages, and terrifies. Losing a child with special needs is so far outside the rules that it bowls you over and mows you down. It's like the double opposite of having your cake and eating it too. There was no cake to not have, and now the cake that never was is gone, and once again, you can't have it. There is just no wrapping your mind around this.

Right after Joel died, I donned a suit of invincible armor and tempted fate by purposely ducking under ladders, jumping into the path of black cats, and stepping on sidewalk cracks. I read Joel's horoscope and scoffed. I laughed in the face of authority and even dared one policeman to hurry up and hand over the ticket he was writing for a dead kid's mom. I developed a wicked sense of gallows humor and a deadpan, forgive me, delivery. Then I laughed and reassured people who cringed at my boldness.

With Joel no longer needing any help, I frantically plied organizations, friends, and family with my assistance. I counseled bereaved parents, advised other special needs families, and provided free strategic guidance for any new business I encountered. I refused to hold still, and everyone called me very strong. I was far from strong—just running as fast as I could. Activity was the default setting that got me out of the door, kept me honest, and held my demons at bay.

I learned that you can run, but you can't hide. All that racing around only served to bring me late to grief. Joel's death is old news, but I can easily relive the day he died in minute detail.

Visions of the orange EMT blankets, closing the eye that was stuck open, holding his fingernail-bitten hand all make me sob and shiver—perhaps a good thing in that I never once cried or shook when it happened. What remain most difficult are the little horrors that land on my brain's doorstep. Rumi tells us that all "guests" are sent for a reason; so, I sometimes allow the miseries to stay and visit. When I do, I begin to digest the fact that there will never be another new photo of Joel. I understand that we will never again hear his deep, nasal voice call out for a "group hug." I accept that his courier bag is empty for good, that his Air Cadet wings are grounded, and that his model bus, plane, and train collections are complete as they stand. Even so, at our Passover Seder I always set Joel's wine cup next to the one for Elijah…and when we open the door for him, I squeeze my eyes shut for a split second, and then open them hoping Joel just might show up.

I have gotten used to the fact that in the midst of a perfectly good day, my head can suddenly reverberate with thoughts that ricochet without warning: Has Joel grown a beard? Is winter colder underground? Has he turned completely to dust, or are any parts of him still left intact? Am I crazy or has Joel actually come back to visit in the form of the dog that vacuums down dinner, burps, routinely knocks into furniture, and ambushes us at the front door just exactly as Joel used to?

Insight is a gift often delivered in a disguise and well past its best before date. In honor of Joel's life and in recognition of his death, I feel an urgent need to use what I have learned before it expires—to be kinder, to feel fortunate, to see the birds, to listen well. Joel showed me that patience and impatience demand the same amount of energy, and that efforts to be the former can be far more productive. His special needs forced me to consider his unique point of view as well as my own and certainly broadened my worldview.

Living with Joel, with his death, and now living without him have taught me that perspective is everything. While his disability initially blinded me into seeing a full glass as half empty, ironically his death now allows me to see an empty glass as half full. The events and initiatives created in his memory, and the notion that nothing bad can ever happen to him ever again, have spun me around, altered my perspective, and protected me.

I am like the paper clip on the helium balloon string, suspended in the numbness of midair.

Thankfully, sadness and happiness continue to register, but oddly, neither to its original degree. When I am low, I find myself somehow safely sad, content, and confident that I will come through it because I have before. There may or may not be a light at the end of the tunnel, but if you pay attention in that darkness, you may be rewarded with some worthwhile shafts of light.

Before Joel's life and death, happiness and excitement were my twin emotions—hard to tear apart, but who cared because they felt so good? These days my happy times are quieter and more subdued...burnished rather than shiny. Even the word *happy* sounds too bubbly for the contentment my current pleasant feelings bring on. I can see now that I can be delighted without being delirious, and I am very grateful for that.

Finally, I have come to believe that Joel's legacy is bound up in the combination of his early death and his challenged, yet accomplished, life. I am better for having known Joel, and perhaps even for having lost him.

PARTING THOUGHTS
June 2019

Looking back, I believe I created *Since Joel* so that I could capture his story by writing him into my head and my heart. I had an awful dream right after he died where he was swirling away from me, sucked and spun through an old sci-fi-movie-type vortex. A friend told me it represented his soul leaving earth and flying up to heaven. To me it just meant he was going to be out of reach forever. In an effort to "keep" him, I began to write down as much about Joel as I could remember so I would be able to read about and recall him as time passed into a future without him.

I have been privileged and challenged by mother-hood. Courtesy of Jonathan's "normal" development and Joel's exceptionalities, I have lived both sides of the parental coin; and each of my sons has taught me much of what I know. With Joel gone, I am left with a hard-earned, but perhaps useful, perspective that comes from having raised and lost a child with special needs.

The notion of highlighting any specific "lessons learned" never sat well with me because if I am so smart, why is my kid dead? After all, who am I to offer advice? On the other hand, regardless of our outcome, I have decided that if any of what I learned might be helpful to others, I am humbled to share some of that.

Here, for whatever they might be worth, are some things that are true for me:

Information is only information until it is pieced together and kneaded into knowledge.

Knowledge is only knowledge until it gets some of that secret sauce called experience—and then it can turn into wisdom.

Fair rarely means equal, but both should always be based on mutual respect.

A good, deep (but time-limited) wallow in self-pity is not a sign of weakness, but rather an acknowledgment of reality.

Denial is more than just a river in Egypt. It pays to name the issue, stare it down, and be reminded that the complaint department is almost always closed for lunch.

On that note, it is better to use energy to make stupid people look smart than to complain about their stupidity.

Since "how things are presented is how they are received," be mindful of where your words will land before you let them fly. Regretful about my swearing episode with our pediatrician, I learned to ask myself, "Who will thank you for this?" before I opened my mouth.

Collecting allies is just as easy as making enemies; so try engaging with positive partners along the path. Better to be viewed as an advocate who is an ally than to be seen as an oppositional solution seeker.

There is nothing funny about having a child with special needs. Yet very few challenges require a better sense of humor. Here is where it turns out that irony can be as much a friend as an enemy.

As exhausting as it may be, where there is life, there is hope. As exhausting as it can be, where there has been death there can also be hope.

ABOUT THE AUTHOR

JULIE SCHWARTZ was born in Philadelphia, the City of Brotherly Love. There she met a Canadian, and forty years ago moved to Toronto and learned to spell her married name with a "zed." Julie earned a Masters and Bachelor of Arts from the University of Pennsylvania. Julie's professional career was as Vice-President and Research Director of a major international advertising agency. Her maternal occupation as the mother of a child with an ASD was devoted to understanding Joel's thoughts, feelings, and actions, and translating him to the community. Now retired, Julie actively pursues outdoor adventures, continuing education, and volunteer opportunities. *Since Joel* is her first book.